FEEDING *your* B·A·B·Y

FROM CONCEPTION TO AGE TWO

LOUISE LAMBERT-LAGACÉ

SURREY BOOKS
230 East Ohio Street
Suite 120
Chicago, Illinois 60611

FEEDING YOUR BABY: From Conception to Age 2
is published by Surrey Books, 230 E. Ohio St., Suite 120,
Chicago, Illinois 60611.
Phone: (312) 751-7330.

This book is manufactured in the United States of America.

Completely revised and re-set. Second edition (first U.S. edition).

Originally published in Canada: Les Editions de l'Homme (French);
  Stoddart Publishing Co. (English)

Library of Congress Cataloging-in-Publication Data:

Lambert-Lagacé, Louise, 1941–
    [Comment nourrir son enfant. English]
    Feeding your baby/Louise Lambert-Lagacé. –2nd ed., rev.
      204 p.   cm.
    Translation of: Comment nourrir son enfant.
    ISBN 0-940625-37-7
    1. Children–Nutrition.   2. Infants–Nutrition.   I. Title.
RJ206.L26413   1991
649'.3–dc20   90-24147
                                                      CIP

Illustrations by Marie-Claire Lagacé

Editorial Production: Bookcrafters, Inc., Chicago
Book Design: Hughes & Co., Chicago
Cover Photography: Michael Brosilow, Chicago
Cover Design: Laurel DiGangi
Typesetting: Pam Frye Typesetting, Des Plaines, Ill.

Single copies of this book may be ordered by sending check or
money order for $12.95 (includes postage and handling) per book
to Surrey Books at the above address.

This title is distributed to the trade by Publishers Group West.

Contents

Introduction

I really could have used a book such as this one when I first became pregnant 29 years ago. I had nausea, was constipated, hardly gained any weight, and had loads of questions about myself and my baby. The only nutritional advice I received from my doctor was decidedly limited: I should eat a piece of cheese every day about as big as an egg yolk. It was up to me to decide whether or not to breast feed and figure out how to do it.

After the birth of a premature daughter weighing 4 lbs. 2 ozs., the only readily available source of information was a very patient pediatrician. Every day he received my innumerable questions, which even Dr. Spock's "bible" could not answer.

I fed my babies without having much information on the most appropriate foods or when to offer them. I struggled through problems of regurgitation, diarrhea, hunger strikes. I imagined all kinds of strategies to get my three little girls to swallow a few mouthfuls of green vegetables. Mealtimes were not always enjoyable.

When I began working as a dietitian, I realized that the anguish and anxiety I had felt during those early years of motherhood were shared by very many women. Stimulated by this, I became professionally involved in infant nutrition, and for the past 15 years, I have gathered, filed, and studied all available information and have shared this knowledge with parents and health professionals.

I am convinced that the quality of the foods served to a baby and the atmosphere surrounding his or her meals are determining factors in future health and eating behavior. Good or bad eating habits are formed long before school days begin.

Many research teams have looked at nutritional needs during pregnancy and lactation, infant foods and supplements, and a score of other issues. This first American edition of my book contains the latest information available on breast milk, breast feeding, infant formulas, and infant foods. The nutritional advice is based on the 10th edition of *Recommended Dietary Allowances* (1989) and the 1990 Institute of Medicine report on nutrition during pregnancy. Questions of the nineties are not those of the eighties. New preoccupations include the ongoing saga of pesticide residues in foods, the challenge of an early return to outside work, food allergies, and meatless meals.

1

In order to have a better idea of these and other current preoccupations of parents and health professionals, my associates and myself collected opinions both formally and informally through surveys during the fall of 1989 and the summer of 1990. The most common worries still center around the introduction of solid foods, the preparation of these foods, what to feed, when to feed, and how much to feed. What milk to choose after six months, what supplement is needed, and what to do with a fussy eater were other prime issues of concern.

From an almost total absence of information in the sixties, we have progressed to an overabundance of advice. Books, magazines, radio and television programs all talk about infant nutrition but rarely transmit the same message. What does one do when, in addition, the pediatrician, the nurse, and the grandmother also disagree? How can you regain faith in your own judgment, in your instinctive expertise without risking errors that could harm the baby?

I really believe that a mother's good common sense is rarely wrong, providing it is based on universally accepted beliefs such as the uncontested advantages of breast feeding, the benefits of a slow introduction to solid foods, and a menu composed of the most naturally good, minimally processed foods.

Infant feeding issues are as complex as cardiovascular disease issues: no single, unique truth exists, no single, unique prescription is possible, no definitive answers prevail. However, during the past ten years, various credible organizations, representing opinions of a large number of experts, have published recommendations concerning infant nutrition. When the Nutrition Committee of the American Academy of Pediatrics and the National Research Council deem it necessary to issue guidelines, when reputable research teams measure the impact of solid foods on sleep patterns of infants, it is important for dietitians such as myself to listen and to adjust the message so that mothers will become less confused and more confident in the way to go.

Feeding your baby well is much more than giving her or him the exact foods and nutrients at the right moment. Feeding your baby well implies an overall strategy that will allow your baby to enjoy eating the most nutritious foods on the market. It also means respecting baby's appetite, food moods, and preferences, thus opening the door to the pleasure associated with eating.

In this book I have expressed my own philosophy of infant feeding while also communicating in plain language the results of current scientific research. The goal is that you better understand both your baby's needs and current recommendations.

I dedicate this book to my three daughters, to new parents, and to parents to be and wish that you may acquire through it a deep-rooted confidence in your own personal abilities to nourish your baby with the healthiest foods.

1
Good Nutrition Means Healthier Babies

Let me share with you my thoughts on good nutrition during the first years of life and then give you a broad overview of the actual impact of sound nutrition practices on your baby's total health. You will find more detailed information in other chapters of this book. Don't worry if I seem to glance over some of the important issues in this introductory chapter.

Good nutrition is the result of a careful feeding program based on top-quality foods given in adequate quantities to insure maximum development and growth, according to your infant's own genetic potential. It implies many hours of tender loving care. It respects the infant's nutritional needs, appetite, digestive capacities, likes and dislikes. It nurtures a positive attitude toward eating. It uses a very basic tool: the best food available!

This is surely the ideal program every parent would like to follow and a very logical first step toward life-long healthy eating. But perfect guidelines written in books are not always possible to follow in real-life situations. I believe in compromise and do not consider an alternative solution as a failure. After all, parents try their best to be perfect, but nobody's perfect all the time.

The keys to good nutrition in the first years of life are numerous and varied. Some may affect your own way of eating, some provide short-term solutions to specific problems, but most are long-term eating strategies. None of the basic principles is really difficult to apply and all work toward a healthier baby.

Good nutrition begins long before birth, with proper diet and weight gain during pregnancy. You can even envisage a *pre*conception diet, beginning three to six months before becoming pregnant, depending on your health and lifestyle. Good nutrition continues after birth with the exclusive use of the best infant food on the market, breast milk, or an appropriate formula. Then follows a slow introduction to solid foods at around four to six months and a sure introduction of texture and variety before the end of the first year. These recommendations comply with recent statements made by the American Academy of

Pediatrics. They are widely accepted and followed by the majority of health professionals throughout North America.

Good nutrition is common sense. Feeding your baby the best food available at the right time does not imply a complicated scientific procedure. The classic studies done by Dr. Clara M. Davis in the late twenties and early thirties confirmed that newly weaned infants could rightly choose their own foods in such quantities as they desired from a fairly wide range of natural foods, unmixed, unaltered, and unseasoned. One of the experiments lasted six to twelve months and involved three hospitalized infants who did very well when only offered "foods that supplied in abundance all the nutritional elements known to be required for good health and sound growth such as high-grade proteins, fresh fruit and vegetables, eggs, milk, and whole-grain cereals." Such an experiment could not be replicated in a home setting because very few parents would agree to offer a daily selection of 33 different foods! But the message remains loud and clear: feed your baby the best food in its most natural state, respect his or her appetite at all times, and optimum growth and development will be ensured.

Good nutrition makes a difference! The use of breast milk as the first food is unanimously recognized as the best choice. It benefits the infant not only because of its exceptionally well adapted nutritional content but also because of its great capacity to reduce infections during the first months of life.

The slow introduction of solid foods at around four to six months allows your infant to swallow more efficiently and digest more easily, and it also retards risks of allergies. The slow introduction of whole cow's milk once the infant is eating 12 tablespoons of solid foods per day decreases problems of dehydration and anemia.

Good nutrition is not synonymous with dieting during the early years. More children are obese today than 20 years ago, but in 90 percent of all cases, a heavy baby at birth does not become a fat baby at 12 months, and a fat one-year-old does not necessarily become an obese adult. It is nonetheless advised in families where the father or the mother, or both, have severe weight problems, to monitor the rate of weight gain quite closely between 12 months and school age and to make proper adjustments when weight gain is excessive during preschool years.

Research on rapidly multiplying fat cells has been done mainly on animals. Very few experiments have been carried out on humans.

What we know is that there are several periods of intense fat cell multiplication during childhood and adolescence and that this multiplication is greatest during the first 12 months. We also know that susceptible infants can become overweight while eating no more calories than normal-weight infants. The problem is not a simple one, but irreversible obesity at one year is a myth whereas normal weight at the end of adolescence is a sure route to long-term normal weight.

Before 12 months of age, there are no scientific reasons to limit the food intake of a fat baby. Possible side effects of such restriction include nutritional deficiencies, reduced spontaneous physical activity, lowered body temperature, and reduced resistance to infections. There is even a danger in offering skim milk during the first year of life. The best way to control overweight during that period is to avoid forcing a child to eat while enticing him into regular physical fun activities. This practice also translates into more parent-child interaction, which is eminently desirable. Other mild measures to prevent overweight can be taken during the second year of life, although they will usually affect the living and eating habits of the whole household.

Good nutrition improves the outcome of gastrointestinal disturbances. When constipation becomes a problem once solid foods are introduced, offering more fluids in between feedings and adding a small amount of insoluble fiber can help produce softer stools. When severe diarrhea occurs, proper refeeding can prevent dehydration and hasten recovery.

Good nutrition can reduce the risks of cardiovascular problems. In a family "at risk" (one in which the father, mother, or grandparents have had cardiovascular problems or an extremely high blood cholesterol level before age 50), prevention with a low-saturated-fat diet is indicated from the earliest years but not before the age of two. By offering a toddler foods rich in soluble fibers (oatmeal, beans, fruit, and vegetables), and by limiting foods rich in saturated fats (meats, processed meats, butter, high-fat cheeses), the formation of irreversible plaques can be delayed and serious problems perhaps avoided.

Good nutrition can prevent iron deficiency anemia. Too many infants still suffer from iron deficiency anemia during the second half of the first year of life. By providing foods rich in iron after six months (iron-fortified infant cereals or iron-fortified formula when appropriate) and foods rich in or enriched with vitamin C at every meal, you can prevent this deficiency. Once the child is eating 12 tablespoons of solid food each day, limiting the volume of whole cow's milk to 32 ounces per day is also important.

Good nutrition prevents tooth decay and other serious dental problems. By avoiding the use of a pacifier covered with honey or another sweet substance and by avoiding giving a bottle of juice, milk, or sugared water at bedtime, the tragic problem of rampant caries is less likely to occur.

By rationing, if not avoiding, the consumption of sweets, particularly between meals, and by showing your child at an early age how to brush his teeth regularly, dental caries will be greatly reduced.

May I conclude this first chapter by saying first that the above list of benefits from good nutrition is by no means exhaustive. Secondly, some of you would like to believe that good nutrition during the first 12 months will provide life-long immunity from major diseases. Sad to say, it doesn't quite work that way. Sound eating practices need to be maintained for many years to obtain long-term health benefits.

Finally, good nutrition is not only a preventive tool to avoid diseases. Good nutrition is also a health-investment strategy for tapping into the top-quality energy found in good-tasting and healthy foods.

2
Good Eating Habits
Lead to Happier Eaters

As previously mentioned, good nutrition is the result of a careful feeding program based on top-quality foods given in adequate quantities to ensure maximum development and growth, according to your infant's own genetic potential. Such a feeding program becomes the cornerstone on which to build your child's long-lasting eating habits. Good nutrition is so closely connected to healthy foods that children need to be raised in the spirit of this connection.

Good eating habits are not developed in the classroom or in the gymnasium. They go back to our first eating experiences and become implanted in our memory for the rest of our lives. Remember for one moment the flavors you really enjoy, the meals you dream of, the foods you always want to avoid, the foods you detest. Can you really separate these eating habits from your early years?

We learn to enjoy food around the kitchen table, in a family setting, in a particular environment. We associate foods with certain rituals, with special celebrations, with happy moments.

A child who consumes fried foods and sweets between TV commercials, who never sits down to eat a real meal, who refuses fruit and vegetables but adores cookies or fruit-flavored beverages does not have the same eating memories as a child initiated to healthy foods in the very first years of life. It is natural for a child exposed to unflavored yogurt, raw broccoli, broiled fish, brown rice, or whole-wheat bread to be happy with such foods. It is excruciating for some adults to convert to these healthy foods after a lifetime of junk eating. A child learns to love good food through various non-verbal messages, positive attitudes toward eating, and exposure to the healthiest foods.

Food can become the attempted solution
to all problems

Fed when hungry, an infant is physically satisfied. Cuddled in your arms while breast fed or formula fed, he is emotionally satisfied. For all babies, physical and emotional satisfaction become associated with meals and with maternal affection. The child responds to two distinct needs, hunger and affection, but these needs can eventually be confused by the baby if you are not careful.

The baby who is fed whenever she cries or is overfed to make her sleep longer cannot tell the difference after a few weeks between the need to eat and other needs. Food becomes the solution to all needs: the need for attention, the need for affection, the need for diversion.

For several years, Dr. Hilde Bruch, a renowned psychiatrist, tried to shed some light on specific eating disorders such as bulimia and anorexia. She found a link between these problems and early childhood experiences. When such disorders develop, food fails as an answer to hunger. Food is used almost exclusively to deal with other problems such as the following:

- desire for inaccessible love
- need to express rage or hatred
- ascetic refusal
- lack of sexual gratification
- protection against growing up and becoming responsible
- a false sense of power

Based on many years of research, Dr. Bruch stresses the need to properly train the hunger mechanism so that it develops appropriately. A baby is not necessarily born as either a big or a small eater. He learns to be hungry when it is time. He learns to know when to stop. He can easily unlearn very early in life.

An infant who is forced to finish a bottle does not learn to control his appetite. A baby who nurses for more than 40 minutes does not learn to control his appetite. A child who is forced to clean his plate is not learning how to control his appetite. They are only learning to obey. You can help your baby from the very first weeks of life to recognize his or her body needs and to satisfy them appropriately.

It takes two to recognize satiety

You and your baby both have a role to play in the normal development of your baby's hunger mechanism.

At birth, your newborn baby is not totally dependent. He can express his needs and desires within the first few hours of life:

- he can cry, cough, swallow, vomit
- he can smell and hear
- he can distinguish between touch and pain

— he can turn his head in the direction his cheek
is touched
— he can twist and kick his feet.

You can help your baby develop by responding to his actions and
reacting correctly to his messages, thus allowing him to become aware
of his potential to communicate his feelings and limits. If you feed
your baby to appease all his cries or to console and comfort him,
you are not interpreting correctly your baby's messages. If you offer
food in reply to a real cry of hunger, you contribute to the development of your baby's hunger mechanism. The right reaction at the
right moment is one of the key factors influencing your baby's eating behavior.

If your baby refuses to drink the last ounce of formula, why insist? Your baby is trying to tell you his limit: he has had enough.
If you respond to his message of satiety, you are helping him develop his own sense of satiety. If not, you are passing along the message of acceptable overeating.

If your baby refuses meat or vegetables when you start introducing solid foods, let him have his way, but do not necessarily give
up on that particular food. Offer it with another meat or vegetable
and see how he reacts. His acceptance of new foods can develop quite
gradually and require all your patience and understanding. Forcing
him to swallow green beans, for instance, is showing a lack of respect for his message of distaste. After all, we all have our own
whims. We like some vegetables and hate some!

When your baby loses his appetite, never force him to eat. His
health is not in danger. Appetites normally vary throughout the first
years of life, and usually an appetite drop coincides with a period
of decreased growth rate. If you understand and react correctly to
the messages your baby sends you at every meal, you enable him
to participate actively in the feeding process.

Food alone is not enough

Total environment plays a vital role in the proper development of
even a house plant. Water and light are not the only factors that make
it thrive. Total environment also affects your child's growth and development and can go beyond feeding the right amounts of foods.
Affection from loving family members needs to supplement the daily
menu and is essential to the most favorable environment.

The association between food and the socio-affective environment
has been the subject of considerable research in Latin America, in

studies looking for ways to minimize the effects of malnutrition on young children. One of these studies looked at weight gain and the health status of two groups of infants living in the same village of Guatemala. One group received supplementary foods for the first six months while the control group did not. The supplemented babies came from larger, poorer, and less-educated families. They gained less weight and were sick more often during the six-month period than the non-supplemented babies. The extra food did not compensate for the lack of human interaction these babies endured in their disadvantaged environment. This extreme example shows the contribution value of attention and affection to the total nourishment of a baby.

Another study showed a definite association between the nutritional status of young children and the extent of communication that went on with their mother. The more often the mother and child interacted using sounds and words, the better the nutritional status of the child. Total nourishment goes beyond food.

Mealtime is critical

Meals are social moments to share food, ideas, and feelings. Meals eaten alone are often meals without pleasure. We adults are very much aware of that reality but tend to forget that young children also enjoy company at mealtime. Taking part in a family meal becomes the child's first social activity. Eating may be the only privileged moment available to see and talk to a working mother and father.

Meals are supposed to favor relaxation, but eating with small children can sometimes become erratic. Meals should not be used as an excuse to quarrel or argue. Such a tension-filled atmosphere can easily affect a young child's appetite. If mealtime is associated with battle time, a child will gradually develop a negative attitude toward food.

Eating problems are not infrequent in early years. They are part of the child's overall development and usually reflect the child's general attitude toward life! Professor A.S. Neil, well-known author of *The Free Children of Summerhill,* says that with a child, an eating problem embodies a certain element of protest. The child uses food preferences at the table to proclaim: I'm the boss here, listen to me.

If you fall into the trap of a power struggle over food, mealtimes will never be fun times, and eating habits will suffer.

Healthy foods become fun foods

Adults that have bypassed healthy foods all their lives do not have much fun eating meatless meals or whole grains. Children raised on healthy foods do not have this problem. Children are born imitators and will readily enjoy the foods adults enjoy around them.

- — If you regularly serve vegetables of all colors and shapes, raw or cooked, your child will accept them much more easily;
- — If you express special appreciation for spring's first asparagus, summer's fresh string beans, autumn's bounty of squash and eggplant, you are helping your child develop a positive attitude toward these foods;
- — If you regularly prepare fish and shellfish of all kinds, your child will not resist seafood experiences and will easily go beyond frozen fish sticks or breaded fish cakes;
- — If you use fresh fruit in season for daily desserts, your child won't feel miserable without a cake, a pie, or a dozen cookies to end a meal;
- — If you prepare meals without meat as a normal occurrence, your child will welcome a great variety of vegetarian dishes.

If you enjoy healthy and tasty foods, you will have no difficulty selling these good things to your child. Good eating habits will develop with ease and pleasure. Your child learns to eat by observing you eat. Actions speak louder than words. She can appreciate the taste of a fresh orange without knowing the merits of vitamin C. She can enjoy broiled liver without knowing about the necessity for iron. Your goal is to have a happy, healthy eater, not a junior nutritionist!

To illustrate the point, let me repeat what I overheard the other day at the supermarket. A young boy in front of the vegetable counter was telling his friend: "I really enjoyed spinach until my mother told me it was good for me."

A child raised to enjoy healthy foods is a happy eater.

3
Good Nutrition Before and During Pregnancy

The recipe for a bouncing and healthy baby contains more than two cups of love and two cups of hope! Many other ingredients affect the final product. Such ingredients include your health status, your lifestyle, your weight before becoming pregnant, and your eating habits during the nine months of pregnancy. This chapter discusses briefly each of these issues and provides up-to-date guidelines so you can adjust your menu appropriately.

Did you know that 35 percent of potential birth defects originate in the first eight weeks of pregnancy and cannot be modified by improving prenatal care? This means that you have everything to gain by making sure your nutritional status is in good shape before you become pregnant. In fact, both parents should be in good general health to increase the chances of a healthy outcome even if mother always has a bit more of the prenatal responsibility.

5 points to consider before pregnancy

1. If you are using an oral contraceptive agent, you should choose another birth control method for at least four months prior to the time you wish to become pregnant. Oral contraceptives appear to have a negative effect on several nutrients, including B vitamins and zinc. By choosing a less invasive method, you allow your body to return to a better nutritional status.

2. If you consider yourself on the slim side, not to say underweight, check the Healthy Weight Chart at the end of this chapter. If your Body Mass Index (BMI) is less than 20, you need to put on a few pounds. Your body needs a certain amount of fat to menstruate and ovulate normally. A study of 26 underweight women with unexplained infertility showed that 24 became pregnant once they reached their normal body weight. Having an appropriate weight at conception means having a BMI between 20 and 26. It is very important to adjust your preconception weight if you want to give birth to a normal-weight baby. If you can't reach your goal before you become pregnant, you need to gain weight very early in pregnancy.

3. If you enjoy social drinking, start reducing your alcohol intake in order to refrain from drinking when you become pregnant. No safe levels of alcohol intake have been established during pregnancy, and possibly serious negative effects on the fetus are shown to be irreversible. The fetal alcohol syndrome, which affects one to two infants per 1,000 live births in the United States, is characterized by growth retardation, distinct facial anomalies, and mental deficiency. Alcohol does not only affect the central nervous system but it impairs the action of such important nutrients as protein and zinc.

4. If you smoke, this is a great time to take a wise decision. You can't dream of having a better motivation! Quit as soon as possible or seriously cut down the number of cigarettes you smoke each day. You should also avoid smoke-filled environments. It can be done! The National Natality Surveys indicate that among American pregnant women aged 20 or older, the proportion of smokers has declined from 40 percent in 1967 to 25 percent in 1980. My own mother, who has been a heavy smoker all her life, has honestly tried to stop at least 50 times since my birth but admits that she only once succeeded in cutting out all cigarettes: for nine whole months during her single pregnancy! It can be done, and it is worthwhile.

Cigarettes have all kinds of side effects. Before pregnancy, they may lower your levels of vitamin C, vitamin A, and folic acid. During pregnancy, smoking retards the growth of the fetus by reducing the blood and oxygen flow to the placenta. No wonder cigarette smokers have a greater incidence of premature and smaller babies, and more complications at delivery.

5. If your eating habits are average but not that good, start choosing foods of higher nutritional quality, giving priority to foods rich in iron and zinc, two key ingredients that can help initiate a healthy pregnancy. To achieve that objective, fill up on whole grains of all kinds from brown rice to whole-wheat pasta, encourage bran cereals, include in your weekly menu a new liver recipe or a dozen fresh oysters, sprinkle wheat germ on fruit, vegetables, and yogurt, and include plenty of vitamin C-rich fruits or vegetables at every meal.

Improving the nutritional content of your menu at this time is ideal. You can enjoy all kinds of new foods and recipes and build up your nutritional status before there is any sign of nausea or fatigue. You are committing yourself to a healthier pregnancy!

Nutritional care before you become pregnant is a way of making sure that the baby's fetal environment is sound and safe. Nutritional care during pregnancy is actually responding to the fetus' needs for growth and development.

The outcome of pregnancy greatly reflects the way you treat yourself, healthwise, stresswise, and foodwise. The foods you eat during these nine months help you produce a complete and healthy human being. It is quite a challenge. Even in our medically sophisticated society, the birth of a healthy baby remains a victory. Although a great majority of mothers meet the challenge with success, still too many give birth to low-birth-weight babies with accumulated risks of handicaps.

In the United States, the infant mortality rate has declined from 29 per 1,000 births in 1950 to 10 deaths for 1,000 live births in 1990, but these are still improvable statistics. To improve the situation, the government has subsidized many programs, including nutrition intervention programs. Why? Because scientific research has shown for years that good nutrition can be effective in preventing prematurity, low birth weight, and infant mortality.

By providing nutrition counseling and extra-nutritious food to needy pregnant women, the Women, Infants, and Children (WIC) program initiated in 1974 has become a success story. The evaluation shows that across the U.S. good advice and good food given to half-a-million low-income pregnant women each month increased birth weight of their infants, reduced the number of low-birth-weight babies, reduced the infant mortality rate, improved the nutritional status of the mother, and improved the infant's growth.

Nutritional care during pregnancy is the obvious route toward a healthy baby. It includes several steps that may or may not require major eating modifications, but each step is relevant to all pregnancies.

Adequate weight gain is fundamental

Times have changed. A pregnant woman in the fifties could barely eat without remorse. She feared both the scale and the scolding from her doctor. She was allowed to gain 15 to 18 pounds and often gave birth to a small baby with many complications.

In 1970 the Committee on Maternal Nutrition of the National Research Council came out with a recommendation urging pregnant women to gain around 24 pounds. Since then, women have gained more weight during their pregnancy and have given birth to heavier, healthier babies.

In 1990 the Institute of Medicine of the National Academy of Sciences emphasized even more the importance of appropriate weight gain during pregnancy. These experts refined the recommendation, using the mother's Body Mass Index (BMI), called the Health Weight, as the initial criterion to determine the appropriate weight gain. Weight gain will vary according to your own weight when you become pregnant. The slimmer you are, the more weight you will need to gain in order to produce a healthy baby. Check the Healthy Weight Chart at the end of this chapter, and find your BMI according to your actual weight at conception.

- If you are quite thin (your BMI is below 20), your weight gain should be between 28 and 40 pounds.
- If your weight is normal (your BMI is between 20 and 26), your weight gain should be between 25 and 35 pounds.
- If you are heavy (your BMI is between 26 and 29), your weight gain can go from 15 to 25 pounds.
- If you are obese (your BMI is over 29), your weight gain can be at least 15 pounds.
- If you expect twins, a weight gain of between 35 and 45 pounds is consistent with a favorable outcome.
- If you are short (less than 62 inches), try to reach the lower end of the target weight gain.
- If you are very young (not yet 20 years old), strive for the upper end of the target weight gain.

All this fuss about weight gain is not just a passing trend. On the contrary, these recommendations stem from years of observations and research that clearly demonstrate that weight at birth generally reflects the mother's weight gain during pregnancy. It has also been observed that inadequate weight gain during pregnancy is associated with a higher incidence of prematurity and higher incidence of low birth weights. The World Health Organization considers that a baby weighing less than 5½ pounds at birth is less likely to survive and develop in good health than a baby weighing 7 to 8 pounds at birth.

All the extra pounds put on during the nine months are very well used. Some of you might think that part of the weight gain goes directly to the baby while the excess remains on your hips. The distribution is slightly more complex.

One-third of the weight gain does go directly to the baby. The other two-thirds are used for auxiliary services: the enlargement of the uterus, which provides the fetus with a made-to-measure lodging; the maintenance of the placenta, which serves as an efficient canteen;

the increase of the surrounding amniotic fluid, which becomes a water bed. The mother's blood volume increases by 33 percent; tissues and breasts also increase in size to ensure better nutrition before and after birth. Only a few pounds remain on the mother—to facilitate her recovery after delivery and to provide sufficient energy during breast-feeding. In round figures, the weight gained in nine months is distributed as follows:

Fetus	7 to 8 lbs.
Placenta	at least 1.5 lbs.
Amniotic fluid	at least 2 lbs.
Uterus	at least 2 lbs.
Breasts	at least 2 to 3 lbs.
Blood volume	at least 3 lbs.
Tissue fluids	at least 3 lbs.
Fat deposits	varies from 6 to 10 lbs.

A regular and gradual weight gain during the nine months corresponds more favorably to the fetus' and the mother's needs than a large but irregular gain.

Even if the fetus' growth is slow during the first trimester, the energy required for the internal reorganization of the mother's body, referred to as the auxiliary services, should not be underestimated. If your weight is normal, a gain of approximately 3.5 pounds in the first three months, followed by a weekly gain of 1 pound, seems adequate. If you are thin, work toward a 5-pound gain during the first three months, and maintain a full pound gain per week thereafter. If you are very much overweight, a 2-pound gain is sufficient in the first trimester, and a 1½-pound gain every two weeks seems adequate for the remaining time.

Pregnancy is absolutely not the time to go on a weight-reducing diet. A menu containing less than 1,800 calories per day can deprive both the mother and the fetus of essential nutrients. Even if you are quite overweight, you need to gain at least 15, and up to 25, pounds if you want to avoid future problems.

An adequate weight gain is a key step to having a healthy baby.

A nutritious menu is a must

At present, you are actively involved in producing a baby, but you must also want to protect your own health and body stores. You are certainly dreaming of being in fine shape for delivery and for the demanding postpartum months. Good nutrition can help you achieve these goals, but good nutrition is often missing on women's agendas.

Surveys done in the United States in the past decade show that many non-pregnant women lack two vitamins and four minerals in their daily diet. Other surveys indicate that pregnant women do even worse. They usually are missing four vitamins and four minerals: vitamins B6, D, E, folic acid, iron, calcium, zinc, and magnesium.

Pregnant women don't seem to realize that they have added responsibilities to accommodate. Their nutritional needs are greater than at any other period of their lifetime, lactation being the only exception.

The recommended daily intakes during pregnancy, as expressed in the latest *Recommended Dietary Allowances* (1989 edition), suggest additions all the way:

Calories:	add 300 calories more each day
Protein (usually 46–50 grams);	when pregnant: 60 grams
Vitamin D;	when pregnant: 400 International Units (IU)
Vitamin E (usually 8 mg);	when pregnant: 10 mg
Vitamin C (usually 60 mg);	when pregnant: 70 mg
Thiamin (usually 1.1 mg);	when pregnant: 1.5 mg
Riboflavin (usually 1.3 mg);	when pregnant: 1.6 mg
Niacin (usually 15 mg);	when pregnant: 17 mg
Vitamin B6 (usually 1.6 mg);	when pregnant: 2.2 mg
Folic acid (usually 180 micrograms);	when pregnant: 400 micrograms
Vitamin B12 (usually 2 micrograms);	when pregnant: 2.2 micrograms
Calcium (usually 800 mg);	when pregnant: 1200 mg
Magnesium (usually 280 mg);	when pregnant: 320 mg
Iron (usually 15 mg);	when pregnant: 30 mg
Zinc (usually 12 mg);	when pregnant: 15 mg

You may forget this list of nutrition jargon, but do not forget the message: a pregnant woman needs more calories, protein, vitamins, and minerals than ever before!

It is surprisingly easy to convert these figures into adequate amounts of food. Simply serve yourself larger portions of top-quality foods. You will get the extra calories and more of all the needed nutrients.

> — To get 300 extra calories each day, gradually add to your menu: 18 ounces of 2 percent milk or 10 ounces of fruit-flavored yogurt or ½ cup raisins and 2 tablespoons of nuts or a peanut butter sandwich on whole-wheat bread.

— To get at least 60 grams of protein per day (many
nutritionists recommend 80 grams), plan to eat
each day: 4 ounces of meat, poultry, or fish; 1
quart of milk or its equivalent in dairy products;
and 4 portions of whole-grain cereal products
(cereal, brown rice, whole-wheat bread). To
limit your total fat intake, choose leaner cuts of
meats and partially skimmed milk. To limit pollutants such as PCBs and dioxins, choose ocean
or farmed fish, the smaller and younger, the better. Avoid fresh-water fish from contaminated
areas.

If you are lacto-ovo vegetarian, you also need at least 60 grams
of good protein each day. Make sure you include in your menu at
least 1 cup of cooked legumes (beans, chickpeas, lentils), 1 quart
of milk or its equivalent in dairy products, 1 egg, 6 portions of whole-
grain cereal products (brown rice, cereal, bread), and 3 tablespoons
of nuts or seeds. The list of foods may seem long, but if you check
the protein chart, you will find that you need all of this to get an
adequate supply of protein.

If you are a vegan, or strict vegetarian, you need to choose high-
quality protein of plant origin to compensate for the absence of animal protein. To obtain approximately 70 grams each day, you need
at least 1 cup of cooked legumes (beans, chickpeas, lentils), 1 quart
of soy milk, 6 portions of whole-grain cereals, 5 tablespoons of nuts
or seeds, and 2 tablespoons of nutritional yeast.

Check the Protein Chart at the end of this chapter.

— To get 1,200 mg of calcium per day, you have
many choices: the easiest consists in drinking
1 quart of milk a day. If milk is not your cup
of tea, you can plan to eat each day 2 ounces
of hard cheese (mozzarella, Edam), 12 ounces
of yogurt, and a bowl of cereal with 6 ounces
of milk. Low-fat milk, low-fat yogurt, and low-
fat cheese contain as much calcium as whole-
milk products. Choose according to your needs.

— If you cannot tolerate milk products or if you
are a vegan, or strict vegetarian, you need to
include in your daily menu: 1 quart of soy milk,
1 generous cup of cooked broccoli, and 4

tablespoons of ground whole sesame seeds. This only provides 750 mg of calcium, so you must add a supplement of 500 mg of calcium with vitamin D.

Check the Calcium Chart page at the end of this chapter.

Other foods contain calcium, for instance, canned fish eaten with the bones, tofu, cooked soybeans, beet greens, and swiss chard, but it seems somewhat unrealistic to count on these same foods day after day.

·Apart from liquid milk, few foods contain any significant amount of vitamin D. That is why you need to include vitamin D with your calcium supplement if you never drink milk.

— To get 30 mg of iron each day, you need to take a supplement beginning in the fourth month of pregnancy. Many foods are rich in iron, but this recommended amount cannot reasonably be met by diet alone. You can obtain 30 mg of iron in compounds such as 150 mg of ferrous sulfate or 300 mg of ferrous gluconate or 100 mg of ferrous fumarate. It is better to take the supplement on an empty stomach, in-between meals, or at bedtime to facilitate absorption. If you have stomach problems with the regular iron supplements, try a liquid drop form called Fer-in-sol, recommended for infants and more easily tolerated by adults.

Even if you are taking an iron supplement, you should not neglect food sources of iron such as:

3 ozs. of liver (chicken, beef, calve's)	7–13 mg
6 medium oysters	5 mg
1 cup cooked legumes (soybeans, lentils)	3–8 mg
3 ozs. of clams or trout	3–4 mg
3 ozs. of cooked lean meat	3 mg
1 cup cooked spinach or swiss chard	4–6 mg
¾ cup bran cereal	5–6 mg
1 cup of prune juice	3 mg

To facilitate iron absorption from foods, serve a vitamin C-rich fruit or vegetable at every meal.

To keep up with other key nutrients during pregnancy, make sure you recognize and eat other top-quality foods.

Excellent sources of zinc include oysters, liver, legumes, and wheat germ.

Excellent sources of magnesium include legumes, dark leafy vegetables, whole-grain cereals.

Excellent sources of vitamin B6 include legumes, liver, whole-grain cereals, bananas, and prune juice.

Excellent sources of folic acid include liver, legumes, sunflower seeds, whole-grain cereals, green vegetables such as asparagus, broccoli, Brussels sprouts, spinach, and fruit such as avocado, orange, and grapefruit.

Excellent sources of vitamin E include polyunsaturated oils (wheat germ oil, sunflower oil, safflower oil, and corn oil). Other sources include dark, leafy vegetables and almonds.

Top-quality foods are "winning foods," especially for you. They provide generous amounts of vitamins and minerals in one single serving!

Milk and milk products provide at the same time: protein, calcium, and vitamin D.

Whole grains provide at the same time: iron, protein, magnesium, vitamin B6, folic acid, and fiber. When possible, choose organic grains and cereal products to decrease your intake of pesticide residues.

Dark green and leafy vegetables provide iron, magnesium, and folic acid. When possible, choose organic leafy vegetables to decrease your intake of pesticide residues. If not available, wash leaves thoroughly.

Legumes provide protein, iron, magnesium, zinc, vitamin B6, folic acid, and fiber. Legumes have a very limited exposure to pesticides, so you need not worry about the residues.

Liver provides protein, iron, zinc, vitamin B6, and folic acid; choose liver from certified organic chickens if you wish to limit overall residues.

If you have never cooked legumes, start gradually with one new recipe a week. Prepare more than needed for one meal, and freeze extra servings for the following week.

You can prepare marvelous pasta recipes from fettucine to lasagna, with spinach or swiss chard and wonderful seasonings.

The daily use of whole grains is a must. Whole grains not only provide the extra fiber everyone recommends but contain three times more magnesium than their refined, enriched counterpart. Whole-grain breads and whole-wheat pastas are now quite easy to find and so flavorful. Oatmeal and oat bran cereals have never been so popular; rich in soluble fibers, they provide a basis for numerous recipes. Brown rice is also easy to find and cook.

These winning foods belong in your daily menu and can make a difference. Your nutritious menu may look like this:

In the morning:

Half a grapefruit or an orange (rich in vitamin C)
Bran cereals with milk or soy milk
   or
Cooked oatmeal with ground almonds and milk
Whole-grain bread or muffin
Milk

At noon:

Broccoli soup or green-pepper salad (rich in vitamin C)
Cheese or salmon sandwich on whole-grain bread
Fresh fruit in season

Snacks:

Milk, soy milk, or yogurt
   or
Cheese and whole-wheat crackers

In the evening:

Carrot sticks or other raw vegetables
Broiled chicken or chickpea casserole
Swiss chard in the wok with brown rice or whole-wheat pasta
Whole-wheat bread
Berries, cantaloupe, or citrus fruit (rich in vitamin C)

To plan similar menus, your daily checklist may be the following:

1. At least 4 servings of milk or milk products or at least 1 quart of soy milk.
2. At least 1 serving of meat, poultry, or fish or at least 1 cup of cooked legumes.
3. At least 5 servings of whole-grain cereal or whole-grain products.
4. At least 1 fruit or vegetable rich in vitamin C at every meal and 1 serving of a dark green or leafy vegetable each day.

This checklist guarantees the nutritional quality of your menu, but you are responsible for adjusting the quantities according to your needs so that you can reach your adequate weight gain.

As you can see, these menu suggestions and eating priorities are quite compatible with the official Dietary Guidelines published by the U.S. Departments of Agriculture and Health and Human Services. They are adapted to your greater nutritional needs during pregnancy and are easy to follow.

Bon appétit!

Appropriate fluid intake is important

Having an adequate fluid intake is a healthy practice at all times. Drinking enough water every day keeps many problems away. But women do not only drink water! Recent U.S. surveys show that 57 percent of young women drink alcohol on a regular basis and that 39 percent of pregnant women continue to drink some alcohol during pregnancy and 3 percent are heavy drinkers. Special care must be taken during pregnancy to limit high-risk beverages.

Alcohol is never a safe beverage, but it is especially unsafe during pregnancy. It is recognized as a powerful promoter of birth defects. What is called the "fetal alcohol syndrome" affects one to two infants per 1,000 live births in the United States. The syndrome is characterized by growth retardation, distinct facial abnormalities, and mental deficiency. Alcohol seems to interfere with normal nutrient absorption and utilization. The damage done in early months of pregnancy is irreversible. No safe levels have been established. It is therefore recommended to avoid drinking alcoholic beverages of any sort throughout pregnancy. What you can drink from time to time is alcohol-free beer or wine, and have fun without guilt!

Caffeine is an active ingredient contained in coffee, tea, chocolate, cola drinks, and many non-prescription drugs. Caffeine stimulates the central nervous system and the cardiac muscle. It passes very quickly through the placenta to the fetus, but the fetus is not capable of dealing efficiently with the substance. Some research studies published in the last ten years have shown that significant caffeine intake is associated with a reduction in birth weight and an increased risk of low birth weight. In 1980 the U.S. Food and Drug Administration recommended that pregnant women avoid caffeine-containing products or use them sparingly. Until further studies delineate an appropriate intake, it appears sensible to limit caffeine daily intake to no more than 300 mg during pregnancy.

Check the Caffeine Chart at the end of this chapter.

If you are very sensitive to the effects of caffeine, you may want to avoid it completely. If you wish to continue drinking coffee or tea, use less and/or brew or steep it for a shorter time to decrease the caffeine content. You can choose among caffeine-free, grain-based beverages; safe ingredients include barley, malt, figs, chicory, or carob powder.

Herbal teas can be enjoyable and healthy warm beverages during pregnancy. Most are caffeine-free. Very few are unsafe during pregnancy. Rosehip, mint, lemon balm, raspberry, and strawberry leaf present no problem. Ginger tea has even been shown to be soothing when you have nausea. Because of lack of safety testing, avoid herb tea mixtures, and favor one herb at a time in a filtered tea bag when possible. Avoid herbal teas that have potentially harmful side effects; these include lobelia, sassafras, comfrey, pennyroyal, devil's clawroot, rue, scotch broom, and goldenseal.

Diet soft drinks contain aspartame as a non-nutritive sweetener. In use since 1982, this sweetener is a recent addition to our traditional diet, and long-term studies of its effects are not yet available. The American Dietetic Association recommends moderation in the use of all non-nutritive sweeteners, especially during pregnancy.

Fruit juices, water, and milk remain your best bets!

Supplements can be useful

An iron supplement providing 30 mg of ferrous iron is recommended daily for all pregnant women, beginning in the fourth month of pregnancy. This amount is provided by approximately 150 mg of ferrous sulfate, 300 mg of ferrous gluconate, or 100 mg of ferrous fumarate. Many pregnant women neglect taking the iron supplement because of side effects such as gastrointestinal pain or constipation. To avoid such discomfort and to make sure that you get adequate iron, try a liquid iron drop such as Fer-in-sol, usually recommended for babies. This form seems much easier to tolerate than other supplements.

A multivitamin and mineral supplement can be useful when you are expecting more than one infant, if you are a heavy cigarette smoker, or if you feel that your menu does not contain a sufficient number of the winning foods listed on the menu checklist above. This supplement should provide approximately:

>   30 mg of iron
>   15 mg of zinc
>   2 mg of copper
>   250 mg of calcium

2 mg of vitamin B6
300 micrograms of folate
50 mg of vitamin C
200 IU of vitamin D

For better absorption, take this vitamin and mineral supplement between meals or at bedtime.

A vitamin D supplement, providing 400 IU per day, and a vitamin B12 supplement, providing 2 micrograms per day, are needed if you are vegan, or strict vegetarian.

A calcium supplement, providing 500 to 600 mg per day, is recommended if you are under 25 years old and do not take enough calcium-rich foods.

Avoid taking a vitamin A supplement that provides more than 10,000 IU per day, especially during the first three months. This vitamin is toxic when taken in excess and can cause birth defects.

Special problems are not infrequent

Eating well during pregnancy is sometimes difficult, especially during the first three months. The slowing down of the digestive process and an increased production of hormones are most favorable to the fetus but can temporarily upset your well-being.

Nausea afflicts as many as half of all pregnant women. Vomiting occurs less often but is even more unpleasant and exhausting. These conditions rarely last more than three months and do not affect the pregnancy outcome. But what a nightmare while it lasts.

Fool-proof solutions are rare, but the following tips can help you find some relief:

— take a soda cracker or a piece of whole-wheat toast before getting up in the morning;
— avoid getting up in a rush in order to minimize sudden movements that can upset the stomach;
— avoid liquids at mealtime; drink in-between meals only, at least 30 minutes after eating solid foods;
— eat more often; try taking five or six small meals per day instead of three big ones; encourage healthy snacks every two to three hours;
— avoid fried food, coffee, and alcohol.

Constipation is another frequent problem during pregnancy. The reason is that the gastrointestinal system works more slowly to allow more time for food particles to be transformed and absorbed. The result is increased absorption of all nutrients. This adaptation process favors the fetus but does not promote regular and easy maternal bowel movements. To compensate for this natural phenomenon, increase your fiber intake and drink plenty of water or juice. You will rapidly feel the difference by just adding one to two tablespoons of natural bran to your cereal in the morning and another tablespoon in your tomato juice and on your yogurt at night.

Planning your postpartum (after childbirth) menu

During the last month of pregnancy, while you are feeling good and have some spare time, plan your menus for the first weeks after the delivery. These postpartum weeks can be hectic and leave you very little time and energy to prepare nutritious meals. Notwithstanding, your nutritional needs are even greater when there is extra stress, less sleep, and more anxiety because of the new baby. It is no time to neglect your menu. Here are a few tested strategies:

- cook and stock in the freezer some of your favorite recipes: meat loaf, macaroni and cheese, spinach quiche, sauces for pastas;
- roast half a turkey, divide the cooked meat into meal portions, and freeze until you are ready to toss a salad, make a sandwich, or bake a casserole;
- stock up on frozen pizza shells, whole wheat if possible; at the last moment, add sauce, mushrooms, peppers, and grated cheese;
- bake whole-grain muffins and freeze for easy and healthy snacks.

This look-ahead cooking strategy can make a big difference when you come back from the hospital. Mealtime won't be a worry, and healthy foods will be at your disposal.

Healthy Weight Chart, or Body Mass Index (BMI)

Height \ Weight (Pounds)	100	105	110	115	120	125	130	135	140	145	150	155	160	165	170	175	180	185	190	195	200
4 ft 9 in	22	23	24	25	26	27	28	29	30	31	33	34	35	36	37	38	39	40	41	42	43
4 ft 10 in	21	22	23	24	25	26	27	28	29	31	32	33	34	35	36	37	38	39	40	41	42
4 ft 11 in	20	21	22	23	24	25	26	27	28	29	30	31	32	33	34	36	37	38	39	40	40
5 ft	20	21	22	23	24	25	26	27	28	28	30	31	32	33	33	35	35	36	37	38	39
5 ft 1 in	19	20	21	22	23	24	25	26	27	27	28	29	30	31	32	33	34	35	36	37	38
5 ft 2 in	18	19	20	21	22	23	24	25	26	26	28	28	29	30	31	32	33	34	34	36	36
5 ft 3 in	18	19	20	20	21	22	23	24	25	26	27	28	28	29	30	31	32	33	34	35	36
5 ft 4 in	18	18	19	20	21	21	22	23	24	25	26	27	27	28	29	30	31	32	32	33	34
5 ft 5 in	18	18	19	20	20	21	22	23	23	24	25	26	27	28	28	30	30	31	32	33	33
5 ft 6 in	18	18	19	19	20	21	21	22	23	24	24	25	26	27	27	28	29	30	30	32	32
5 ft 7 in	17	18	18	19	20	20	21	22	22	23	24	24	25	26	27	27	28	29	30	31	31
5 ft 8 in	17	18	18	19	19	20	21	21	22	22	23	24	24	25	26	26	27	28	29	30	30
5 ft 9 in	17	18	18	19	19	20	20	21	22	23	24	25	25	27	28	29	29	30			
5 ft 10 in	17	17	18	18	19	20	20	21	22	23	24	24	25	26	27	27	28	29			
5 ft 11 in			17	18	18	19	20	20	21	23	24	25	26	27	27	28					
6 ft					16	17	17	18	18	19	19	20									

1. Find your height in the left-hand column.
2. Find your weight at the top of the chart.
3. Circle the point where they meet. That is your BMI.
4. Compare your BMI with the following information:
   - 20 to 25 corresponds to the "healthy weight."
   - 26 to 28 is an intermediate zone, tending toward overweight.
   - More than 29 indicates obesity and an increased risk of disease.
   - Less than 20 enters the thin zone, and can also correspond to an increased risk of disease.
   - A woman who is 5'5" tall and who weighs 110 pounds has an index of 18 and weighs less than her healthy weight.

- A woman who is 5'1" and weighs 130 pounds has an index of 25 and is within the range of her healthy weight.
- A woman who is 5'6" and weighs 135 pounds has an index of 23 and is within the range of her healthy weight.

Any active woman between the ages of 20 and 80 can calculate her Body Mass Index (BMI). However, a growing teenager, a pregnant woman, a nursing mother, an athlete, or a woman over the age of 80 cannot interpret these figures in the same way since her body composition is different.

Chart taken from *The Nutrition Challenge for Women*, Louise Lambert-Lagacé, Bull Publishers, 1990.

Protein Chart

Intake of 60 grams of protein per day is your goal
(Many nutritionists recommend 80 grams)

4 ozs. of meat, poultry, or fish . . . . 28 gr
1 qt. of milk or its equivalent in dairy products . . . . . 32 gr
4 portions of whole-grain cereal products
   (cereals, brown rice, whole-wheat bread) . . . . 12 gr

If you are lacto-ovo vegetarian,
you also need at least 60 grams of protein

1 cup, at least, of cooked legume products
   (beans chickpeas, lentils) . . . . 15 gr
1 qt. of milk or its equivalent in dairy products . . . . . 32 gr
1 egg . . . . 7 gr
6 portions of whole-grain cereal products
   (brown rice, cereal, bread) . . . . 18 gr
3 tbsps. of nuts or seeds . . . . 9 gr

If you are a vegan, or strict vegetarian,
choose high-quality protein of plant origin

1 cup, at least, of cooked legumes
   (beans, chickpeas, lentils) . . . . 15 gr
1 qt. of soy milk . . . . 28 gr
6 portions of whole-grain cereals . . . . 18 gr
4 tbsps. of nuts or seeds . . . . 12 gr
2 tbsps. of nutritional yeast . . . . 6 gr

Calcium Chart

1200 mg of calcium per day is your goal
when pregnant and nursing
(800 mg ordinarily)

Using milk products:

1 qt. of milk .... 1200 mg
2 ozs. hard cheese (mozzarella, Edam) .... 400 mg
12 ozs. yogurt .... 600 mg
1 bowl of cereal with 6 ozs. milk .... 200 mg

Not using milk products:

1 generous cup of cooked broccoli .... 200 mg
4 tbsps. ground whole sesame seeds .... 350 mg
1 qt. soy milk .... 200 mg
1 serving of cooked legumes .... 60 mg
1 serving of vegetables .... 44 mg

If your total intake does not come close to 1200 mg:

A calcium supplement with vitamin D is needed

Caffeine Chart

300 mg of caffeine per day limit when pregnant

Beverages	Caffeine mg in 7 oz.
Soft Drinks	
Regular	23–42
Diet	21–35
Caffeine-free	.08
Coffee	
Instant	82–94
Percolated	130–166
Dripolated	182–204
Flavored	58–122
Decaffeinated	6–10
Bagged tea	
Black, 5 min. brew	56–72
Black, 1 min. brew	30–48
Loose Tea	
Black, 5 min. brew	58
Black, 3 min. brew	50
Green, 5 min. brew	30
Iced Tea	12–26

Chocolate	Caffeine mg
Bar (1 oz.)	5–20
Baking (1 oz.)	45
Cocoa/hot (7 ozs.)	8–14
Syrup (2 tbsps.)	10–17

Medications	Caffeine mg per tablet
Non-prescription	
Aspirin compounds, Bromo-Seltzer	32
Cope, Midol	32
Excedrin, Anacin	32–60
Dristan, Sinarest	30
No Doz	100
Vivarin	200
Pramaline, Dexatrim	140–200
Coricidan	32
Prescription	
APCs (aspirin, phenacetin, caffeine)	32
Darvon compound	32
Migral	50

4
Breast Milk Is Best

You are getting ready for baby's arrival, planning your schedule for the coming months, finding a good babysitter, part-time help, or adequate day care. You may not have made a final decision concerning your choice of milk for your baby. This is such an important decision that I encourage you to take your time.

Read this chapter attentively and learn about the benefits of breast milk for you and your baby. Discuss the issue with your partner and see how he feels about breast-feeding. Visit or phone friends, family members, or acquaintances that have already breast-fed; ask them all the questions you have on your mind. Ask your doctor or the clinic nurse if there is a support group in your community for breast-feeding mothers. Once you feel comfortable with all the answers, make an honest decision. Even if you come to the conclusion that breast-feeding for you cannot last more than a month or two, it is worth all the effort.

Breast milk is the best milk for your baby because it is marvelously adapted to her needs. Since the beginning of history, it has been recommended for all babies. Unfortunately, it has been underestimated and partly set aside by a few generations of parents during this 20th century.

The most recent U.S. surveys indicate that 52 percent of mothers breast feed when leaving the hospital, and 22 percent breast-feed until five months. Health authorities hope to see the percentages increase by the year 2000 to 75 percent of mothers breast-feeding at birth and 50 percent at five months.

For the past 20 years, numerous scientific studies have been conducted throughout the world, helping us rediscover the overall attributes of human milk. Science is filling a knowledge gap while groups such as La Leche League International compensate for the lack of cultural support in our present society. Scientific research is giving us facts and widening our comprehension concerning this exceptional food while support groups help us rediscover the "how to do it."

Now we know that breast milk is adapted to each species, and that its main ingredients vary depending on the needs of each species. The protein content varies according to each mammal's growth rate.

The higher the protein content of the milk, the faster the species grows. For example, a horse doubles its birth weight in 60 days and drinks a milk with 2 percent protein. A rabbit doubles its weight in 6 days and drinks a milk with 12 percent protein. A calf doubles its weight in 50 days and drinks a milk with 3.4 percent protein. A human baby doubles its weight in approximately 150 days and receives a milk with 1 percent protein.

The protein and mineral content of the milk has an impact on the number of feedings needed in 24 hours. The denser the milk, the longer the interval between each feeding. Mice produce one of the most diluted milks of all species and spend 80 percent of their time feeding their young. Rabbits produce a very dense milk and feed their young only once a day. Humans produce a less concentrated milk and need to feed their baby several times a day.

The fat content of the various milks is related to the size of the animal and to the environmental temperature of his natural habitat. The larger the animal and the colder the environment, the higher the fat content of the milk. Thus elephant's milk contains 20 percent fat, seal's milk 43 percent, and that of the blue whale is 50 percent fat.

The carbohydrate content of the milk varies according to the rate of brain development after birth. Accordingly, human milk contains more carbohydrate, in the form of lactose, than any other milk.

Nature has thought of everything. The kangaroo, which carries in its pouch two young of different ages at the same time, produces two types of milk; the younger animal drinks a more concentrated milk from one nipple, and when the older one nurses from another nipple, it receives a more diluted milk suited to its needs. The Hokkaido monkey gives birth in the spring and nurses its young all summer. In the autumn, the mother lets the baby forage for himself and replenishes her own stores. But when snow appears and food is scarce, the young monkey resumes his intake of mother's milk for another season.

If you look more closely at the human infant and his worldly needs from birth on, you cannot fail to acknowledge the many advantages of breast milk. Life after birth is not that easy for your infant. Having been comfortably lodged in your womb at an ideal temperature, fed without effort, your baby now has to take charge of several functions on his own: he has to breathe, maintain a proper body temperature, feed himself, digest and eliminate the food, fight against infections, and so on. The transition period between life as a fetus and life as an infant in the outside world requires more than a balanced diet. It demands a delicate combination of food and love. Breast-feeding can fulfill this unique challenge. It supplies all the nutrients your baby needs, provides very special protection against infection, and at the same time transfers loads of warmth and affection.

Breast milk has unique nutritional qualities

The main components of breast milk are marvelously adapted to the infant's needs. The colostrum, which is the yellowish liquid secreted during the first days after birth, has less calories and less fats but more protein, vitamins, and minerals than mature milk. It is very rich in antibodies and responds to the needs and the reserves of the newborn at birth. No other formula can provide this initiation drink.

The transitional milk secreted during the second week of life has less protein, more fat and lactose than the colostrum, but the calorie content is slowly increasing to respond to the infant's needs.

The composition of the mature milk varies during the day, even during a feeding, but the major components have definite characteristics.

The protein content of human milk is much easier to digest than proteins in cow's milk or other infant formulas. Once in the stomach, these proteins coagulate into easily digested, miniature particles that are well absorbed by the infant, unlike the harder and larger protein particles found in cow's milk. Present in the right proportion, they are very well suited to the infant's needs.

The fat content, or fatty acids, in human milk do not only provide calories but greatly contribute to the development of the infant's brain. During the first months after birth, 20 percent of the brain cells continue to multiply. A full 60 percent of the solid matter of a human brain is composed of subproducts of essential fatty acids. Human milk contains adequate amounts of the two essential fatty acids, linoleic and linolenic acid; this fulfills the infant's needs much better than cow's milk, which has seven times less. Infant formulas are constantly adjusting their fat content to better imitate breast milk, but even if some supply both fatty acids, they are not as efficiently used as in breast milk.

Another particularity about fat in human milk is that it varies from feeding to feeding. Day feedings are richer than night feedings. Foremilk secreted at the beginning of a feeding has less fat than hindmilk secreted during the last minutes of a feeding. This unique phenomenon favors appetite control in the breast-fed baby and is hardly reproducible in an infant formula.

The cholesterol content of human milk is remarkably stable even if you eliminate cholesterol-rich foods and saturated fats in your own diet. Cholesterol is considered an essential ingredient for the infant.

Investigators indicate that animals fed high levels of cholesterol early in life are better able to cope with cholesterol later in life, and they maintain lower cholesterol levels. No cholesterol is yet found in infant formulas.

Lactose, which is the natural carbohydrate present in milk, is much more abundant in human milk than in any other milk, and for very good reasons. Once it is transformed into galactose, it actively participates in the development of the central nervous system and greatly enhances the absorption of calcium in breast milk. Not all formulas contain lactose.

Iron contained in human milk was previously thought to be insufficient for the infant. Research has shown that this type of iron, even if present in small quantities, is very well absorbed by the infant because of the other components in breast milk. Subsequent surveys have found that breast-fed babies rarely showed signs of iron deficiency anemia compared to babies fed cow's milk or infant formulas. The American Academy of Pediatrics confirmed the effectiveness of iron in human milk a few years back and stated that this iron is quite adequate for a full-term, normal-weight baby until the age of six months or until solid foods are introduced.

Other minerals such as calcium and phosphorus are found in smaller quantities in human milk than in cow's milk, but these amounts are more respectful of the infant's immature renal system and are at the same time sufficient to insure growth and development of the bones and teeth. Human milk contains three times less sodium and potassium than cow's milk. These quantities are better suited to the baby's needs and immature renal system.

Zinc is present in large quantities in the colostrum secreted during the first days after birth. It works toward the infant's overall immunity, and the amount slowly decreases thereafter. This zinc seems better utilized by the infant than the type added to infant formulas.

Selenium is also present in adequate quantities in breast milk if maternal intake is adequate. Some experts suggest that it should be added to infant formulas to prevent any possible deficiency.

Vitamin D is present in small quantities in breast milk and is not influenced by your intake. The biological activity of this vitamin does not always provide effective protection against rickets among infants, especially if the mother is a strict vegetarian or the infant is very seldom exposed to sunshine.

Vitamin C contained in human milk varies slightly, according to the mother's diet. The mammary glands can process some of the vitamin and supply the infant with adequate quantities.

Vitamin A content of colostrum is twice the amount found in mature milk, but the supply remains adequate through infancy.

Vitamins of the B complex are found in sufficient amounts in human milk when the mother is well nourished. Levels respond to dietary adjustments and to supplementation. Mothers who take vitamin B supplements increase the vitamin B content of their breast milk.

A breast-fed infant also receives a sufficient supply of water through the breast milk and does not require extra fluid, even in warm temperatures.

Breast milk provides protection against infections and allergies

It is well known that breast milk protects babies all over the world from all kinds of infections. It lowers the incidence of diarrhea in North America as well as in the Third World. Breast-fed babies in the United States have fewer episodes of respiratory illness and otitis media. If they do suffer from such illnesses, they are not as sick as formula-fed infants and do not become dehydrated. Breast-feeding even on a partial basis appears to protect young infants in day care centers, where the incidence of illness is quite alarming.

During the first few months of life, a baby does not have the built-in resistance to face the whole outside world, a highly contaminated environment. Her defense mechanisms, or immunological system, are only partially completed. That explains why one infant in ten becomes infected during delivery or in the early months of life.

Breast milk supplies an abundant quantity of protective agents during this critical period, especially through the colostrum secreted during the first days after delivery. All protective antibodies in breast milk have specific self-defense roles to play.

All classes of immunoglobulins are present in breast milk and remain active as long as you breast-feed. The concentrations are definitely higher just after birth and generally drop by the third week of life. One of these immunoglobulins, called "sI_8A," is not affected by the stomach's acidity; it remains intact until it reaches the intestinal tract, then lines the intestinal walls with an antiseptic material, helping the baby react against such pathogens as the polio virus and bacteria that could enter the body through the gut.

The bifidus factor is 40 times more abundant in colostrum during the first few days after birth than in more mature breast milk. This factor promotes the growth of intestinal flora that can effectively limit the multiplication of undesirable bacteria. There is a striking difference between the intestinal flora of a breast-fed baby and that of a formula-fed infant; that surely explains the very small incidence of intestinal infections among the first group. It is interesting to note that the bifidus factor is resistant to freezing temperatures as well as very high temperatures.

Lactoferrin is another protective agent that has a strong action against bacteria. It has also been demonstrated to inhibit the growth of *Candida albicans*. Many other immunological agents are secreted in breast milk and provide the infant with unique protection against bacterial and viral infections. No infant formula can provide such a defensive arsenal.

Breast milk is also a powerful tool to help decrease the incidence of infantile allergies. Just after birth, the baby has a very limited capacity to deal with allergenic substances. The intestinal wall is more permeable in these early months so that allergenic foods can penetrate the system more easily, causing all kinds of problems from eczema to asthma. Many studies published in the past ten years support the antiallergenic powers of breast milk. Even if it does not provide guaranteed protection against infantile colic or future allergies, breast milk remains the best preventive measure, especially in families with a history of food allergies. (See Chapter 5 for colic in breast-fed infants and Chapter 9 on food allergies in infancy.)

Breast milk is a vehicle for warmth and affection

Facts are facts! A lactating breast is warmer than a non-lactating breast! Breast milk is more than a nutritious food. It flows from the maternal body into the infant's mouth. It requires close body contact and generates warmth.

The whole breast-feeding process brings with it extra benefits for both you and your baby. It is obvious but it often takes a few scientific reports to confirm the obvious. For several years the scientific community focused on saving infants' lives and assuring them of adequate growth and development. It was the priority. More recently, a few medical teams have started to look at ways to foster stronger parent-child attachment and the more harmonious development of children.

Klaus and Kennel have studied very closely initial parent-child interactions. Struck by the high incidence of abandoned or abused children and by failure to thrive when separation from the parents occurred during the first months of life, they identified a common cause for these sad situations. They found a link between the lack of mother-infant physical contact during the first days of life and a higher frequency of such problems. The less often a mother took her infant in her arms, the less eye contact she had with her baby, the less communication there was between the two, the more developmental problems occurred later.

The minutes and hours immediately following birth are critical times to initiate mother-child interaction. Breast-feeding within an hour after delivery is one way of providing this early and extended contact. The whole breast-feeding process reinforces this mother-child interaction.

It is undoubtedly possible to establish a strong mother-child attachment without breast-feeding your baby, but breast-feeding offers a unique opportunity for closeness from the very first moments of life.

Breast milk is the healthiest fast-food available

Breast milk is always at the right temperature, travels easily, is ready to serve, contains no preservatives, and is always fresh without refrigeration. No other food on earth is that convenient.

Your baby is the winner when it comes to breast milk, but you also reap some benefits. Breast-feeding can simplify your daily routine and save you time and money. No need to buy formula bottles and nipples; no need to wash and warm bottles, care for the nipples, and so on. You can feed your baby anywhere, anytime; you can even combine traveling and mothering, always having the healthiest food on hand.

Breast milk is the most nutritious choice available:

- Proteins are adapted to the baby's needs and are easily digested.
- Essential fatty acids allow adequate brain development, and high fat content at the end of a feeding helps satisfy your baby's appetite.
- Lactose present in large quantities helps develop the central nervous system and enhances the intestinal flora.
- Iron and zinc are very well absorbed.
- Other minerals do not overload the baby's renal system.
- Vitamins A and C are present in adequate quantities.
- Vitamin E is in good proportion to the essential fatty acids.

— Vitamins of the B complex are usually adequate
if your own menu is good; if not, a supplement
can help increase the amounts.

Breast milk fulfills all your baby's needs except for vitamin D, especially lacking if your baby is born in fall or winter months in the northern states. (See Chapter 8 on vitamin supplements.)

Breast milk is affected by the environment

Breast milk is close to perfection, but the pollution in our industrialized countries has had an impact on its content. Several undesirable substances such as DDT, PCBs, dioxins, and pesticides pass into the maternal body, are stored in body fat,* are particularly stable, and can stay there for years; but they can eventually be released in breast milk.

In the case of DDT, the levels found in breast milk have consistently decreased since the North American ban in the late 1960s.

PCBs, originally used in paints, printer's ink, and electrical transformers, were banned by Congress in 1976. No new PCBs are manufactured, but many have remained in the environment to affect mothers and their milk. Since PCBs accumulate in animal tissues of the food chain, our main exposure to PCBs comes from fish from contaminated waters, such as the Great Lakes, and to a much lesser degree from foods rich in fat, such as some meats and cheeses. PCB levels in breast milk are important but do not pose a threat to the baby's health since the exposure lasts only a few months and not a lifetime.

Dioxins and furans, which consist of 135 different toxic substances, mainly originate from the combustion of PCBs, the bleaching of paper, and from incinerators. They definitely accumulate in the food chain, particularly in fish from polluted waters and foods rich in animal fat. They are stored in human fat tissue and are easily released into breast milk. Analyses have shown high levels in breast milk of North American mothers, but higher levels are found in some European countries. Since pollution has a tendency to travel north, the most polluted breast milk is found among Inuit mothers that feed on large quantities of fish from polluted Arctic waters.

Among the 75 identified dioxins, the most toxic one does not seem to accumulate in breast milk, even in the worst scenario, such as exposure to the polluted smoke of a catastrophic PCB fire. In Que-

*This explains why losing too much body fat is not recommended while breast-feeding.

bec province in 1988 milk of mothers exposed to such smoke did not contain more of that dioxin than other samples of breast milk.

Pesticides originate more directly from the food supply and accumulate more readily in foods of animal origin. Foods such as meat, poultry, fish, and butter retain more pesticides than legumes (peas and beans), fruit, and root vegetables. Breast milk from strict vegetarian mothers contains less residues than other breast milks.

A study carried on for 12 months in North Carolina compared breast-fed infants to formula-fed infants and found no correlation between the level of exposure to pollutants and the psychomotor development, growth, and health of the exposed babies. As usual, formula-fed babies had a higher incidence of otitis media and gastrointestinal problems. Another study done on three consecutive generations of rats exposed to contaminated milk with high doses of dioxins (exceeding 100 times the recommended limits) did not show any toxic effects.

You cannot ignore the issue, but environmental pollution should not keep you from breast-feeding if you want to give your baby the best milk available. Considering all aspects, breast milk remains the most nutritional infant food and provides the best protection against early diseases, as underlined recently by the World Health Organization.

Pollution affects not only breast milk. Infant formulas also have their load, containing more toxic metals such as lead and cadmium than human milk. Formulas also retain more radioactive iodine than breast milk, as shown after the Chernobyl incident.

No food is perfect, but breast milk is surely the best for newborns.

(See Chapter 6 on how to limit your intake of pesticides and pollutants while breast-feeding.)

5
The Art of Breast-Feeding

In the early sixties, when I told my doctor I wanted to breast-feed my first baby, he smiled, looked at my husband, and said that I could try for a few weeks. That was the end of the information and support I received. No wonder I did not succeed in fulfilling my dream. Those Dark Ages for breast-feeding are now past history, but you can never be too well prepared for this exceptional experience.

If your mother, a cousin, or a good friend successfully breast-fed, use their expertise to slowly get ready, psychologically and physically. Look for a lactation clinic in your area and consult a lactation counselor even before birth if you feel you need more information or more support.

Make sure your partner feels comfortable with your decision to breast-feed. His encouragement and collaboration during these early months can make a world of difference. Win the approval of the rest of the family so that your living routine with your newborn is well accepted by everyone.

Get organized so that breast-feeding fits in nicely with the rest of your life, or should I say, more realistically, so that the rest of your life fits in with the breast-feeding schedule! No one can deny the extra work load imposed by a newborn during the first few months. Breast-feeding requires even better organization if you want to succeed with flying colors, maintain your energy, and enjoy your baby.

No doubt you can produce milk of good quality, but in order to trigger milk ejection and secrete enough of it, you need to eliminate as much stress as possible—it is your worst enemy! You cannot maintain a superwoman schedule, a tidy house, entertaining activities, and still breast-feed day and night. Develop a short-term breast-feeding life plan, and learn to cut corners short. Set your agenda on your baby's needs and wants, and forget the rest of the world for the first critical weeks or months.

Getting ready during pregnancy

Getting ready may mean buying an answering machine so that phone calls will not bother you when you feed the baby.

Getting ready means buying a brassiere that is adjustable and usable for both pregnancy and lactation. This will give you good support. Once in a while during pregnancy, open the flaps in the front of the brassiere and expose the nipple and the areola under the clothing to experience a gentle, soft abrasion of the surface. Swedish mothers attribute the absence of sore nipples to the fact that they expose their breasts to sunshine and loose clothing routinely throughout young adult life. This is an efficient and quite inexpensive way of conditioning your breasts before delivery, as long as you avoid sunburn, of course!

Getting ready is having a supply of ready-made dinners, snacks, and suppers in the freezer so you need not worry about your meals during the first weeks after delivery.

Getting ready is having parents and friends agree to share some of your housekeeping responsibilities, doing the groceries, entertaining an older child, helping out with homework, walking the dog.

Getting ready is finding the coziest spot in the house for nursing.

If you still have not made your final decision, let me dispel a few other worries you may have.

If you had breast surgery to remove a benign cyst or to increase the size of your breasts, you can still breast-feed successfully in most cases as long as the nipples were not moved. Check with the lactation clinic in your area.

If you have inverted nipples, the most effective antidote is the use of breast shells (plastic or glass) over the nipple and areola inside of your brassiere for six to eight weeks (or longer) before delivery. You may need a larger bra to accommodate the shells. These shells, available through La Leche League International, provide an even, gentle, and constant pressure over the areola, causing the nipple gradually to evert. Continue wearing the shells after birth, between feedings until lactation is well established.

You may have small breasts and wonder if you can adequately breast-feed. Good news! There is no relationship between breast size and the volume of milk produced. In fact, larger breasts hide more fat but not necessarily more milk stores. During pregnancy, the mammary gland network in each breast increases due to hormonal changes, and local milk "factories" are responsible for milk production quite independent of breast size. Confidence in your power to breast-feed seems to have a much greater impact on milk volume than the size of your breasts.

You are worried about your weight. You gained a fair amount during pregnancy and would love to regain your pre-pregnancy figure fast! You heard that "breast-feeding leads to faster weight loss" but new research doesn't quite see it that way. A recent study done in Louisiana followed a group of mothers for six months after birth. Calorie intakes and weights were compared among totally breast-feeding mothers, partially breast-feeding mothers, and mothers who gave infant formula. Breast-feeding mothers ate 2,000 calories per day, lost slowly in the first three months, but came to a total loss of 18 pounds at six months. Mothers who gave formula ate 500 calories less each day and lost a comparable 18 pounds at six months. Mothers who alternated between breast milk and formula ate 2,000 calories per day and lost 16 pounds at six months. As you can see, breast-feeding allows weight loss at a reasonable pace, but to maintain adequate milk production, you cannot lose too quickly. Slower weight loss also helps you maintain a lower level of pesticides in your milk.

If you wish to alternate between breast milk and infant formula, slowly decrease your food intake to respond to your lower energy needs. Pre-pregnancy weight is usually attained by the end of the first year whatever type of milk you choose to give your baby. A sound diet and personalized program of physical activity is safest.

You are worried about losing your freedom. Becoming a parent implies redefining your concept of freedom, finding ways to reconcile your needs while not jeopardizing your baby's. Providing tender loving care to a newborn requires quite a few hours a day, but this new role can become very gratifying. Whatever type of milk you choose to give your baby, your freedom will be limited for some months. If you choose to breast-feed, you can plan free time for yourself once your milk production is well established. Toward the fourth or fifth week, express your milk with a pump or manually, let the father or a friend give baby a bottle, and enjoy the freedom!

You heard of postpartum blues and wonder if breast-feeding can protect you against this depression. Sorry to say, the incidence of this usually short-term depression is the same for mothers who breast-feed as for mothers who formula-feed. The good news is that it only lasts a few days in most cases.

If you need a Caesarean, you can still plan to breast-feed. After a C-section, you produce as much milk as if you had a regular delivery, but you need more time and rest to recover. Plead in favor of local anesthesia so that your baby can develop a good sucking reflex in the first days after birth. Do not hesitate to take medication against pain, but make sure it is not contraindicated. Plan to have your baby live-in if possible, and ask the father to take care of baby while you rest. Slowly find the best position to breast-feed, and ask for all the help you can get.

You are worried about becoming quickly exhausted. This can easily happen if you don't take good care of yourself before and after delivery. Getting enough sleep during the last month of pregnancy, eating winning foods, forgetting about dust and fancy meals can help build your resistance. Nobody denies that giving birth, initiating breast-feeding, and coping with day and night schedules represents a challenge. The first week can be euphoria, even if baby requires many feedings and loads of attention. By the second week, when your baby improves his feeding and sleeping schedule, don't hesitate to take naps whenever you feel like it, snack on healthy foods as often as needed, and listen to inspiring music to maintain your physical and emotional strength.

You've been a junk food/fast-food eater for years and feel you don't have what it takes to properly supply your baby with top-quality milk. Don't worry. The nutritional qualities of breast milk are somewhat independent of your daily intake of nutrients. In Third World countries, mothers who eat little food of sometimes poor nutritional value succeed in producing a breast milk rich in protein, fat, carbohydrate, and immunological substances for at least three months. This kind of milk saves millions of lives throughout the world. Your milk is sure to be good enough. And it is never too late to improve your diet and increase your intake of vitamin-rich fruit and vegetables and good whole-grain cereals! It's easier than you think.

After your baby is born

Try to breast-feed as soon as possible: within the first hour after birth. During that very special hour, your baby is usually wide-awake, actively discovering his new environment and responding to your messages. His sucking reflex is particularly strong. He then falls into a deep sleep and does not cry intensely until the third day. Early sucking triggers breast milk production, and a number of studies have associated successful breast-feeding with this initial feeding, given within the first hour of the infant's life.

Insist on having your baby live-in with you in your hospital room so that you can nurse him on demand. The first days are days of learning and adjustments. Nursing as often as every couple of hours is essential to initiate a good milk supply. Very frequent feedings not only stimulate the production and secretion of milk but provide your baby with plenty of fluids that can help prevent jaundice, a common problem among newborns. Frequent feeding also allows you to respond to your baby's unique needs for warmth and affection.

Find a comfortable nursing position and make sure the nipple is well back in the baby's mouth, with the gums, hard palate, and tongue pressing on the areola. Good positioning is a key to effective breast-feeding.

Begin by nursing no more than five minutes at each breast; offer both breasts at each feeding, starting with the breast offered last at the preceding feeding. Gradually increase the length of each feeding. Never interrupt the baby while he is actively sucking to burp him; wait until he pauses so that he can reject swallowed bubbles.

Give yourself a few weeks to feel really comfortable with your baby and to come to a satisfactory schedule. The entire breast-feeding process is the result of many daily interactions between you and your baby.

Avoid giving your baby a bottle of formula or sweetened water between feedings. This only decreases your baby's appetite and can easily disrupt your milk production. Breast milk provides all the fluids your baby needs even in warm weather.

Although mothers have breast-fed for hundreds of thousands of years, breast-feeding in our society, in isolation and with very little support, has become a challenge. Even with the best of intentions, you may experience problems that seem overwhelming during the first month or so. They most often are not unsolvable. Don't give up. Many solutions are available to help you overcome the problems.

You may feel that the let-down reflex is slow, that the milk flow does not come readily when your baby begins to suck. The let-down reflex is a physiological reaction that causes the release of milk from the breast. Sucking stimulates the hormonal system, which then triggers the flow of milk. This normal reaction evolves over time and may take a few weeks to become consistent.

Once the initial tenderness of the breasts decreases, once you and your baby become more experienced, the let-down reflex will occur much sooner after the baby starts sucking. Don't forget that this reflex is very sensitive to your mood. If you are in a rush, tense, embarrassed, preoccupied, or quite anxious, the reflex can be inhibited. Before you reach the perfect breast-feeding strategy, try applying some heat on the breasts ten minutes before feeding time by taking a bath or a shower or applying a heating pad or hot, wet towel.

If you feel you have insufficient milk you are not the only one! This is the greatest source of worry among breast-feeding mothers. The more often you nurse, the more milk you will produce. You may need to meet extra demands when your baby is hungrier during the second week of life, at around five or six weeks, and at around three months. Increasing the number of feedings will allow you to meet this demand. Never reduce the number of feedings to less than six per day during the first three months.

You most definitely have the power to produce enough milk, but to succeed day after day requires that you take good care of the producer, yourself! Make sure you are eating plenty of healthy foods (see Chapter 6) and drinking plenty of fluids at meals and between meals. Make sure you are resting enough, reducing tension to a minimum. Enjoy the close and warm relationship with your baby and forget the volume of milk.

Your baby's growth is the most reliable way of assessing the adequacy of your milk supply. Ideally, a breast-fed baby gains two pounds per month over the first three months and one pound per month during the following three months. Another way of assessing your milk supply is to keep track of wet diapers: six to eight wet diapers per day usually means your baby is getting enough milk.

If your baby is not gaining weight steadily, consult your doctor and the lactation clinic in your area.

Cracked or sore nipples are not a severe problem but need to be treated promptly. Make sure your baby is well positioned during feeding, horizontal, propped by pillows, and slightly turned toward you. Nurse your baby often, on demand, and make sure the baby sucks properly and swallows. Once the breast is drained, do not let your baby suck; use a pacifier instead. After each feeding, air dry or blow dry nipples before replacing the bra flaps to avoid any dampness. Wash breasts with water only (no soap) and dry carefully. A preservative-free lanolin based cream may be used.

Engorgement may be the problem if your breasts feel hot, hard, and tender with painful swelling. This can happen when more milk is produced that the infant actually takes or when feedings are too far apart. Reconsider your feeding schedule and have your baby feed more often on demand, from both breasts. Express excess milk after a feeding or prior to a feeding to relieve pressure. Take a warm shower or apply a hot, wet towel on the breasts to start the milk flow. You can also massage your breasts to help recirculate the milk flow, pushing left-over milk down toward the nipple.

Mastitis can start like an engorgement but progress into an infection accompanied by fever. Breasts feel warm and some areas become reddish and very tender. This is a signal that you need more rest while increasing the number of feedings to decongest the breasts. If your baby does not suck enough, hand- or pump-express to relieve the pressure. You can try ice chips on your nipple five minutes before feeding to decrease the pain. If the pain is acute, take an acetaminophen (coated aspirin less likely to cause gastrointestinal problems) 20 minutes before nursing. An antibiotic prescription might be necessary but will mean that you must discontinue breast-feeding or that breast-feeding must alternate with formula.

If you think your baby has colic, go over the main symptoms and examine your breast-feeding technique before changing anything. Colic usually begins the second or third week of age and normally disappears before the fourth month. Breast-fed babies are as vulnerable to colic as formula-fed babies. The infant has sudden attacks of pain, a distended and tense abdomen, drawn-up legs, arched back, pushed-out belly, clenched hands, and flushed face; symptoms often get worse after 4:00 P.M. Babies can cry and scream for hours. The cause is not easy to track down: it can relate to poor burping technique, under- or overfeeding, air swallowing, or food intolerance caused by your own diet.

The following techniques may help control colic:

- Start by making sure your baby is in the correct position while breast-feeding to limit air swallowing.
- Feed on demand.
- Make sure the first breast is completely emptied before switching to the second so that your baby receives an adequate amount of fat and energy. A lack of fat can cause symptoms of hunger with crying and fussiness.
- Don't hesitate to rock and cuddle your baby more often.
- Sometimes your baby will respond better if comforted by another person, such as the father or grandmother.

If all this doesn't work, try eliminating from your diet allergenic foods such as milk products or other protein food for at least seven days. If you notice a difference, reintroduce milk products a few days later to challenge the baby's reaction. If the elimination of milk products or protein food works, change your menu, but make sure it is nutritionally adequate. (See menu plan in Chapter 6.)

Even if you tried your best, problems can persist. You may have consulted the best people in your network, and their proposed solutions haven't worked. You may be ambivalent but still have come to the conclusion that you need to quit. The decision is very hard to make and even harder to live with, but you feel that your survival depends on it. Comfort yourself by knowing that you have not failed as a mother. You simply have been unable to fulfill your breast-feeding goal. But even if you breast-fed for only a couple of weeks, your baby has gained unique immunity and you have lived through a unique experience.

Coping with an employment schedule

Employed mothers are routine in our society. A survey of new mothers carried out in the late eighties across the United States showed that 55 percent of fully employed mothers chose to breast-feed their babies, which happens to be the exact proportion of mothers not employed who also chose to breast-feed. Working wives and mothers are the rule nowadays rather than the exception. It is not easy to work and breast-feed, but it can be rewarding if you are willing to give it a try.

Carefully plan your return to work, and use your last weeks of maternity leave to get ready physically and mentally. Your greatest challenge is getting enough rest to ensure an enjoyable and beneficial breast-feeding experience while coping with a more hectic schedule.

Before you go back to work, develop your ability to express your milk, manually or with a pump. Hand-expression can initially require as long as 45 minutes for both breasts, but with practice, the whole operation can take 20 to 30 minutes. Manual pumps are available but are not always comfortable and efficient. Electric pumps are more expensive but very effective and can be rented at monthly rates and left at the office in a very quiet, secure spot.

If you intend to provide your milk for all of your baby's feedings, start building a milk supply a few weeks in advance. You can store it in sanitized glass bottles for two weeks in the freezer compartment of your refrigerator or for up to six months in a deep-freeze.

Make sure your baby is acquainted with a bottle so that she readily accepts it when you are absent.

Spend at least one day with the babysitter, going over your strategy, so that you feel comfortable with your return to work. You can choose to have the babysitter bring the baby to your workplace, you can return home for lunch, or you can work half-days or split shifts.

If you decide to alternate between formula and breast milk, start both types of feedings a week or so before going back to work, and adapt your own system to your new breast-feeding schedule. Continue to breast-feed in the morning, late afternoon, and evenings.

Once you start working, give your ideal strategy a try and see how it works. Don't hesitate to adjust as you go along.

If you need to express your milk at work, find a room with some privacy and express your milk in a Pyrex cup or another container rinsed with boiling water. Pour the milk into a sanitized container or a pre-sterilized nurser bag. Store in refrigerator or in a large pre-cooled Thermos jug. Never leave the milk at room temperature.

Take care of yourself, never skip meals, and never skip breaks! You need all the breaks you can get to cope with a demanding work load.

Make sure your baby is not fed for two hours before you come home so that when you arrive, you can relax and breast-feed. Save your first 45 minutes for the baby. Unhook the phone if necessary, and if possible, recruit helpers for preparation of the evening meal.

If your work environment provides some support, it can make your life relatively easy. The following example can inspire you to improve your own environment. A few years ago, a community hospital made a commitment to promoting breast-feeding among employees. The administration rented an electric pump and made arrangements with employers for nursing mothers to pump their breasts in an appropriate and accessible location during working hours. This simple program was shown to be quite effective in helping working mothers to continue nursing after return to employment.

Your success in breast-feeding while employed greatly depends on your ability to recruit help around you for this very noble cause. Good luck!

6
The Nursing Mother's Menu

You want to enjoy these early months of motherhood as much as possible and build a unique relationship with your baby. You want to feel good and eat properly without putting on weight. You've heard of exhaustion during these first months, you have friends that gave up breast-feeding because of lack of energy. You need a nutritious diet but can't spend hours shopping for special foods or cooking sophisticated meals. Your schedule is hectic and your staff is limited! Your hours of sleep are cut short by a growing baby, craving the best milk on the market.

The recommended diet while you breast-feed is a simple one: no strict rules, no special foods, but a generous menu like the one you adhered to during the mid-months of pregnancy. You have done a fine job of increasing your food and nutrient intake during the past nine months. Apart from the foods you presently eat, your milk production will be subsidized by some of the extra pounds taken on during pregnancy and not lost after delivery.

You are hungrier and thirstier than ever, which is normal. Your nutritional needs are at an all-time high; you need more protein, more vitamins, and more minerals than ever before. To respond to this challenge, choose foods that are filled with nutrients and simple to serve. You can really increase your energy level and your overall resistance by eating top-quality foods and eating more frequently. The first month after delivery, you need at least three meals a day and as many snacks as you wish, especially when you must wait more than five hours between meals and have fewer sleeping hours than ever. If you eat more often, your body burns calories more efficiently, your metabolic rate increases, and normal weight loss becomes easier.

Make sure you include foods rich in protein and rich in fiber at mealtime and snacktime. These two key nutrients allow you to avoid ups and downs, energy-wise and emotion-wise. You will find protein in meat, poultry, fish, seafood, eggs, cheese, yogurt, and milk as well as in beans, legumes, tofu, nuts, and seeds. You will find fiber in plant foods exclusively, such as whole-grain cereals, nuts, legumes, fruit, and vegetables.

A healthy meal contains three types of foods:

— one or more food rich in protein;
— generous amounts of vegetables and fruit;
— one or more whole-grain products.

A healthy snack contains a food rich in protein and a fruit or a food rich in protein with a whole-grain product. Food stores do have many ready-to-serve products that provide good quality nutrients and respect your special needs. Invest in winning foods, those foods that provide plenty of nutrients in every mouthful.

During the first three months of motherhood, forget about stews, pies, and fancy meals. Forget about an ultra-clean kitchen, set aside meal entertainment, and concentrate on the essential, happy integration of the new family member. Recruit helpers for feeding tasks. Ask your mother, a friend, or the father to buy the groceries once you have made the list. No one can refuse to peel a few carrots, prepare a yogurt dip, or make homemade, low-fat granola-type cereal for breakfast.

If you planned for this exceptional period during pregnancy, as suggested (pg. 26), you already have some homemade frozen meals and snacks in your freezer and emergency foods on hand such as almonds, sunflower and sesame seeds, cheese, canned kidney beans or chickpeas, evaporated milk, canned salmon, shrimp or tuna, peanut butter, applesauce, and so on. You can survive without worrying for at least a week. Have you ever thought of asking a good friend to prepare one of your favorite dishes as a gift for the new mother? Depending on the response, you may want to request the same favor from other friends or work colleagues.

A healthy breakfast is nothing complicated:

— a food rich in protein such as milk, egg, yogurt, cheese, or peanut butter;
— a fruit rich in vitamin C, providing approximately 75 mg of vitamin C, such as an orange, a grapefruit, a kiwi, a piece of mango or cantaloupe, or strawberries (the vitamin C enhances iron absorption for the whole meal);
— a whole-grain product such as a bowl of oatmeal, whole-wheat bread, a bran muffin, or a whole-wheat waffle.

For a nutritious bonus, add a sliced banana, a few teaspoons of bran or wheat germ (kept in the refrigerator), raisins and nuts. If you feel more tired than usual, add one to two tablespoons of Torula or Engevita yeast to a glass of milk or tomato juice; this gives you an extra dose of B vitamins.

You can even try a minute breakfast in a glass by putting in the blender 1 fresh fruit cut up in big pieces, 1 cup of plain yogurt, 2 tablespoons of frozen orange juice concentrate, and 1 tablespoon of wheat germ. Mix and drink.

For lunch and supper, serve top-quality protein foods that are ready to eat: cooked chicken, frozen shrimp, canned fish, cheese or tofu, canned kidney beans or chickpeas. Serve liver once a week, if you like it, or other iron-rich foods. (See iron sources in Chapter 3.) Don't forget fruit and vegetables rich in vitamin C, served raw, steamed, or cooked in the microwave with very little water. Encourage dark, leafy vegetables such as spinach and swiss chard to insure a good magnesium intake. Have someone prepare a large batch of vegetable soup; freeze it in freezer bags and build healthy meals around it by adding kidney beans and Parmesan cheese to make minestrone; or add cooked chicken or cubes of tofu for an oriental meal in a bowl!

Prepare salads with the freshest and greenest leaves of the season. Prepare large quantities of salad dressing, using cold-pressed oil and herb vinegar. Keep leftover dressing in the refrigerator. Serve regularly whole-grain bread, whole-wheat pasta, and brown rice with the nutty flavor to get all the fiber and minerals you need. Indulge in bran muffins or homemade oatmeal cookies for extra calories and fun.

Your daily menu

To summarize, your daily menu will contain:

- 4 servings of milk products;
- at least 6 servings of fruit and vegetables, giving priority to the ones that are rich in vitamin C and at least a few times a week to dark green, leafy vegetables;
- at least 5 servings of whole-grain products rich in fiber and many other nutrients;
- 2 servings of protein-rich foods such as meat, poultry, fish, eggs, legumes, or tofu. Avoid fish from contaminated waters; prefer farmed or ocean fish or seafood. One serving is the equivalent of approximately 3 ounces of meat;

— plenty of fluids when you are thirsty but no excessive quantities; 8 glasses of water or juice or other beverages seem adequate;

— 1 to 2 tablespoons of cold-pressed oil; alternate between sunflower oil and olive oil. Do not heat the oil. Serve on salads or on cooked vegetables. Such oils supply good-quality polyunsaturated and monounsaturated fatty acids and some vitamin E.

Consult the 7-day menus at the end of this chapter that are adapted to your needs, with or without meat.

Such daily menus provide between 2,000 and 2,200 calories and allow you to produce an adequate volume of milk. Mothers who have tried to cut calories down to 1,500 per day have significantly affected their milk supply. Some had to quit breast-feeding for lack of milk and energy.

If you decide to alternate between infant formula and breast milk, you can slowly but only slightly decrease your calorie intake, subtracting the equivalent of one serving of whole-grain cereal and one fruit to see how you and your baby feel.

Problem foods during nursing

There are theoretically no problem foods during lactation. However, a few cautions should be taken.

Strong flavored vegetables such as cabbage, onions, and garlic may alter the taste of breast milk but few babies object to new flavors. Experiment and see how your baby reacts before eliminating any such food.

Caffeine found in coffee, tea, chocolate, many cola-based drinks, and some drugs (see Caffeine Chart at end of Chapter 3) stimulates you, and a small percentage does reach your baby. Research has shown that babies cannot eliminate this stimulant very efficiently, and they accumulate caffeine in their system over time. If your baby is calm and sleeping well, don't worry about caffeine as long as you are also calm and sleeping well. If, on the contrary, you would like to see your baby sleep longer hours, try cutting down to a minimum of caffeine-rich drinks and foods; switch to caffeine-free alternatives.

Alcohol can be relaxing at times, but it is rapidly transferred to breast milk. Large quantities of alcohol may even inhibit the let-down reflex and disturb the infant. On the other hand, an occasional glass of beer or wine is quite an acceptable source of relaxation.

Very spicy or salty foods can alter the taste of breast milk and do not really belong in your list of winning foods. Taken very occasionally, they can only surprise your baby.

Fried foods, sweets, and rich desserts can cause digestive problems; you gain no advantage in eating such foods.

Milk products or other sources of protein, such as beef, chicken, or fish, can be allergenic and cause reactions in some infants, especially in families with a history of food allergies. If your baby has colic and has not responded to other strategies, first eliminate all milk products for seven days, and adjust your menu in consequence. If you see no progress, eliminate another source of protein, such as beef, and see how that works.

How to avoid pollutants

You may have already taken safety measures during pregnancy to minimize all environmental pollutants (PCBs, dioxins, and pesticides) in your breast milk. If not, it is never too late to improve the quality of your milk.

Avoid fresh-water fish, especially from contaminated areas. Check with your local health unit. Choose a variety of ocean fish and seafood such as cod, sole, halibut, crab, and haddock or "farmed" fish such as trout and salmon; prefer smaller and younger fish that have less residues.

Avoid fish oils (cod liver or halibut oil).

Choose leaner cuts of meat and trim away fat. Eat chicken without the skin even if you cook it with the skin.

Choose low-fat cheeses when possible.

Avoid crash diets that mobilize pollutants in your fat tissue and favor secretion through your breast milk.

Choose organic whole-grain cereals, leafy vegetables, fruits, and cold-pressed oils when possible. If organic choices are not available, peel the fruit and wash the leafy vegetables especially thoroughly.

Dietary supplements

Vitamin and mineral supplements during lactation can be beneficial. Continue with the multivitamin and mineral supplement you were taking during pregnancy. Your nutritional needs are high, and key nutrients are missing in many women's diets during lactation.

If you need to eliminate all milk products from your menu, replace milk with a soy-protein infant formula or a fortified soy milk beverage, or else take 1,000 mg of calcium each day in a supplement. Make sure your prenatal calcium supplement already contains

400 IU of vitamin D; if not, take a calcium supplement with vitamin D.

If you are lacto-ovo vegetarian and plan your menus with winning foods, no need to worry. Nonetheless, you do gain an advantage by taking a multivitamin and mineral supplement during the lactation period.

If you are a strict vegetarian and eat no food of animal origin, make sure you drink at least four glasses of fortified soy milk beverage each day for good-quality protein and zinc. To fortify your soy milk beverage, add one teaspoon of powdered calcium lactate per glass. Add to your menu one to two tablespoons of blackstrap molasses for extra iron. Nibble on nuts and seeds for calories. To insure your baby's normal growth and development, you also need to take supplements that provide:

- 2.5 micrograms of vitamin B12
- 1000 mg of calcium
- 400 IU of vitamin D

Pay close attention to medication because all drugs rapidly reach breast milk and your infant. Most have little effect on the infant, but some should be avoided. Consult your physician before taking any special drug therapy. Always use the safest oral analgesia, such as acetaminophen instead of aspirin. Reduce the infant's exposure by taking the medication just after a feeding or just before your baby's lengthiest sleep period.

Oral contraceptives taken in low doses do not present a problem once the milk supply is well established, but there remain some concerns over the long-term effects of such steroids excreted in breast milk. Alternative contraceptive methods are recommended such as the use of a condom with or without foam at any time after birth.

A 7-Day Menu for Nursing Mothers*

Day 1

With Meat, Fish, or Poultry	Lacto-ovo Vegetarian
BREAKFAST	
½ grapefruit	½ grapefruit
banana muffin with ricotta or cottage cheese (¼ cup)	banana muffin with ricotta or cottage cheese (¼ cup)
glass of milk or café au lait (8 oz.)	glass of milk or café au lait (8 oz.)
LUNCH	
raw carrot sticks	raw carrot sticks
chunky lentil soup (1 cup)	chunky lentil soup (1 cup)
whole-wheat bread (2 slices)	whole-wheat bread (2 slices)
plain yogurt with fresh or thawed strawberries (4 oz.)	plain yogurt with fresh or thawed strawberries (4 oz.)
SNACK	
fruit and milk (8 oz.)	fruit and milk (8 oz.)
DINNER	
baked chicken breast (3 oz.)	baked pasta, broccoli, and cheese casserole
herbed brown rice	whole-wheat pita bread
steamed broccoli	salad greens
whole-wheat pita bread	fresh pineapple slices
fresh pineapple slices	herbal tea
herbal tea	
SNACK	
milk or yogurt (8 oz.)	milk or yogurt (8 oz.)

*If you are not breast-feeding, forgo the evening snacks but consider this 7-day menu plan as a good postpartum diet.

Day 2

With Meat, Fish, or Poultry	Lacto-ovo Vegetarian
BREAKFAST	
orange juice	orange juice
oatmeal with raisins and milk	oatmeal with raisins and milk
whole-wheat bread, toasted (1 slice)	whole-wheat bread, toasted (1 slice)
milk or café au lait (6 oz.)	milk or café au lait (6 oz.)
LUNCH	
red pepper rings	red pepper rings
grilled salmon sandwich or pita bread stuffed with salmon	1 grilled English muffin spread with peanut butter or cheese
banana	banana
glass of milk (8 oz.)	glass of milk (8 oz.)
SNACK	
fruit juice and cheese (1½ oz.)	fruit juice and cheese (1½ oz.)
DINNER	
brown rice and chicken casserole	brown rice and lentil casserole
steamed zucchini and carrots	steamed zucchini and carrots
gingerbread muffin and orange yogurt (4 oz.)	gingerbread muffin and orange yogurt (4 oz.)
herbal tea	herbal tea
SNACK	
milk or yogurt (8 oz.)	milk or yogurt (8 oz.)

Day 3

With Meat, Fish, or Poultry	Lacto-ovo Vegetarian
BREAKFAST	
quartered orange	quartered orange
muesli-type cereal with milk	muesli-type cereal with milk
whole-wheat bread, toasted (2 slices)	whole-wheat bread, toasted (2 slices)
milk or café au lait (8 oz.)	milk or café au lait (8 oz.)
LUNCH	
salad of cooked and raw vegetables	salad of cooked and raw vegetables
cheese cubes (2 oz.) and nuts	cheese cubes (2 oz.) and nuts
slice of whole-wheat bread or bran muffin	slice of whole-wheat bread or bran muffin
fresh cantaloupe	fresh cantaloupe
milk	milk
SNACK	
milk and dried fruits (8 oz.)	milk and dried fruits (8 oz.)
DINNER	
broiled hamburger (3 oz.)	red kidney beans (1 cup) with herbs and brown rice (½ cup)
coleslaw with apples	coleslaw with apples
slice of whole-wheat bread	slice of whole-wheat bread
fresh fruit salad	fresh fruit salad
herbal tea	herbal tea
SNACK	
milk or yogurt (8 oz.)	milk or yogurt (8 oz.)

Day 4

With Meat, Fish, or Poultry	Lacto-ovo Vegetarian
BREAKFAST	
½ grapefruit	½ grapefruit
shredded wheat with milk garnished with nuts and wheatgerm	shredded wheat with milk garnished with nuts and wheatgerm
whole-wheat bread, toasted (1 slice)	whole-wheat bread, toasted (1 slice)
milk or café au lait (6 oz.)	milk or café au lait (6 oz.)
LUNCH	
vegetable juice	vegetable juice
chopped egg sandwich (1 egg) with alfalfa on whole-wheat bread	chopped egg sandwich (1 egg) with alfalfa on whole-wheat bread
fresh kiwi	fresh kiwi
milk (8 oz.)	milk (8 oz.)
SNACK	
apple and cheese (1 ½ oz.)	apple and cheese (1 ½ oz.)
DINNER	
oven-poached fish fillet (4 oz.)	whole-wheat macaroni & cheese
sliced tomato	sliced tomato
steamed broccoli	salad greens
whole-wheat bread	banana with yogurt sauce (4 oz.)
banana with yogurt sauce (4 oz.)	herbal tea
herbal tea	
SNACK	
milk or yogurt (8 oz.)	milk or yogurt (8 oz.)

Day 5

With Meat, Fish, or Poultry	Lacto-ovo Vegetarian
BREAKFAST	
orange juice 1 egg (soft-boiled or poached) whole-wheat bread, toasted (2 slices) milk or café au lait (8 oz.)	orange juice 1 egg (soft-boiled or poached) whole-wheat bread, toasted (2 slices) milk or café au lait (8 oz.)
LUNCH	
minute minestrone soup with kidney beans (1 cup) whole-wheat bread (2 slices) yogurt with fresh mandarin oranges (4 oz.) milk (8 oz.)	minute minestrone soup with kidney beans (1 cup) whole-wheat bread (2 slices) yogurt with fresh mandarin oranges (4 oz.) milk (8 oz.)
SNACK	
raisins and milk (8 oz.)	raisins and milk (8 oz.)
DINNER	
tomato juice seafood pizza garden green salad applesauce herbal tea	tomato juice vegetarian pizza with cheese garden green salad applesauce herbal tea
SNACK	
milk or yogurt (8 oz.)	milk or yogurt (8 oz.)

Day 6

With Meat, Fish, or Poultry	Lacto-ovo Vegetarian
BREAKFAST	
orange and grapefruit juice	orange and grapefruit juice
shredded wheat sprinkled with nuts, raisins, and milk	shredded wheat sprinkled with nuts, raisins, and milk
whole-wheat bread, toasted (1 slice) or 1 bran muffin	whole-wheat bread, toasted (1 slice) or 1 bran muffin
milk or café au lait (6 oz.)	milk or café au lait (6 oz.)
LUNCH	
green pepper rings	green pepper rings
grilled cheese (2 oz.) sandwich with tomato	grilled cheese (2 oz.) sandwich with tomato
fresh pear	fresh pear
milk (8 oz.)	milk (8 oz.)
SNACK	
fruit and milk (4 oz.)	fruit and milk (4 oz.)
DINNER	
pasta primavera with shrimp	pasta primavera with lentils and sunflower seeds
whole-wheat bread (1 slice)	whole-wheat bread (1 slice)
lettuce-and-spinach salad	lettuce-and-spinach salad
yogurt (4 oz.) and strawberries	yogurt (4 oz.) and strawberries
herbal tea	herbal tea
SNACK	
milk or yogurt (4 oz.)	milk or yogurt (4 oz.)

Day 7

With Meat, Fish, or Poultry	Lacto-ovo Vegetarian
BREAKFAST	
quartered orange	quartered orange
2 bran muffins	2 bran muffins
milk or café au lait (8 oz.)	milk or café au lait (8 oz.)
LUNCH	
vegetable juice	grated carrot salad
tuna and brown rice salad	split pea & barley soup (1 cup)
whole-wheat bread (1 slice)	whole-wheat bread (2 slices)
fresh cantaloupe	fresh cantaloupe
milk (8 oz.)	milk (8 oz.)
SNACK	
raisins and nuts	raisins and nuts
milk (8 oz.)	milk (8 oz.)
DINNER	
stir-fried chicken with vegetables	stir-fried tofu with vegetables
Chinese cabbage salad	Chinese cabbage salad
whole-wheat bread (2 slices)	whole-wheat bread (2 slices)
tangerine	tangerine
oatmeal cookie (1)	oatmeal cookie (1)
herbal tea	herbal tea
SNACK	
milk or yogurt (4 oz.)	milk or yogurt (4 oz.)

Nursing menu without milk products

Plan to eat, every day, the following foods that supply all the needed nutrients, including calcium:

- — at least 3 glasses (24 ounces) of fortified soy milk beverage* or the same amount of soy protein infant formula (Isomil, Nursoy, or Prosobee); use this soy milk with cereal, in soups, sauces, and creamed desserts, and enjoy excellent results;
- — at least 6 servings of fruit and vegetables, including a daily serving of broccoli, collards, swiss chard, or beet greens;
- — at least 5 servings of whole-grain cereals;
- — 2 tablespoons a day of whole, ground sesame seeds; sprinkle over your cereal, on soups, or use as a dip for fresh fruit;
- — 2 servings of protein-rich foods such as meat, poultry, fish, or alternates, including a daily serving of tofu or cooked legumes or canned fish eaten with the bones.

*To a glass of soy milk beverage, add one teaspoon of powdered calcium lactate.

7

Infant Formulas and Other Milks
Before and After Six Months

Even if breast milk is impossible to copy and offers more nutrition than any other infant formula, you can decide not to breast-feed your baby for many good reasons, or you may have breast-fed a few weeks or a few months and wish to offer your baby the most appropriate substitute.

Alternatives to breast milk have been used for centuries, but because of unsatisfactory sanitation practices, they were never available on a large scale. Safe infant formulas are a product of this century and are now being offered to close to 50 percent of U.S. newborn babies. Commercially prepared infant formulas have become the second best choice, the most suitable alternative to breast milk during the first six months of life. Other milks such as ordinary cow's milk, whole, partially or totally skimmed, evaporated milk, or goat's milk are not recommended for a newborn baby.

Infant formulas are essentially designed to fulfill the infant's nutritional needs and constantly undergo modifications to better mimic breast milk, changing contents as often as once or twice a year, depending on the most recent research on breast milk. At least 30 different formulas exist presently on the market from milk-based to meat-based. Before you choose the appropriate formula for your baby, let us go over the main formula categories and their components.

Milk-based infant formulas

Milk-based products include such items as Enfamil, Similac (two different kinds), Milumil, and SMA. They are prepared essentially from cow's milk that has been diluted and processed to approach concentrations found in breast milk. The protein resembles cow's milk protein, with 80 percent casein and 20 percent whey or lactoserum (Milumil, Similac), or the protein imitates breast milk, with 40 percent casein and 60 percent whey or lactoserum (Enfamil, SMA, Similac). Despite these latter modifications, protein in formulas is more allergenic than in breast milk and does not have any anti-infectious properties.

The carbohydrate used in milk-based formulas is lactose, the same type of carbohydrate found in breast milk. Lactose is essential for the absorption of minerals and for healthy tissue growth. Milumil also contains modified starch and glucose polymers, which can be helpful for babies unable to digest large quantities of lactose.

The fat content in these formulas is most often a blend of soy and coconut oils in an attempt to imitate the proportion of unsaturated and saturated fats found in breast milk. The ratio present in formulas does not quite mimic breast milk but most often supplies both essential fatty acids for the on going development of the infant's nervous system. Some formulas do not contain soy oil and provide only one of the essential fatty acids; this could lead to health problems.

The mineral content of milk-based formulas is adjusted to the infant's needs so that it can be properly absorbed. The iron content varies depending on whether you choose a regular or an iron-fortified formula. All milk-based formulas are now available in both forms. The use of an iron-fortified formula is recommended by the American Academy of Pediatrics to help reduce anemia among infants. Contrary to popular belief, babies fed iron-fortified formula do not have more constipation, loose stools, or fussiness than babies on non-fortified formulas. Only the color of the stools differ, being darker and greenish with the addition of iron.

The vitamin content of milk-based formulas is based on the content of breast milk under optimum conditions. The only exception is vitamin D, which is added to prevent the risk of rickets, 400 IU per quart of formula. If not exposed to regular sunshine, breast-fed infants should also receive an additional 400 IU of vitamin D each day.

Milk-based infant formulas meet the nutritional requirements of healthy, term babies and are associated with normal growth and development. Most of them come in three different forms:

- A liquid concentrate is available in cans from food stores and drug stores. Simply add an equal amount of water. If tap water is used, boil it for 20 minutes and cool before mixing with the concentrate. If bottle water is used, choose a "spring water" labeled "sterile," containing a minimum amount of mineral salts.
- A powdered concentrate may be purchased. Mix carefully, using exact measures of powder and water to obtain the proper dilution.
- A ready-to-serve form is also available, with no dilution needed. This is the most expensive

form but quite convenient when traveling with
your baby.

Soy-based infant formulas

Soy formulas include such products as Isomil, Nursoy, Prosobee,
and Soyalac. These formulas are not comparable to commercial soy
milk beverages such as Edensoy and Westsoy, sold as alternatives
to milk in natural food stores. The soy-based infant formulas are fortified to fulfill the infant's needs, which is not the case with regular
soy milk beverages.

Soy formulas are recommended primarily for infants in strict
vegetarian families where no animal products are eaten, and in cases
of lactose intolerance. In cases of cow's-milk allergy, these formulas
may not always be useful; as many as 40 percent of infants allergic
to cow's milk are also intolerant of soy.

The total nutritional content of soy-based infant formulas resembles breast milk. The protein of plant origin comes from soy flour,
which is isolated and then processed into a balanced formulation;
a small amount of L-methionine, an essential amino acid, is added
to improve the quality of the total protein.

The carbohydrate content of soy formulas varies; sucrose is used
in Isomil and Nursoy while glucose polymers are used in Prosobee.
The substitution of other carbohydrates for lactose is appropriate for
babies that cannot tolerate lactose following severe diarrhea or born
with a metabolic abnormality.

The fat content remains a blend of soy and coconut oils such as
those found in milk-based infant formulas. The vitamin and mineral
content meets the infant's needs.

These soy-based formulas are available in liquid concentrate or
powdered form. To prepare, you need to take the same precautions
as for a mild-based formula.

Protein-hydrolysate-based formulas

These are found in products such as Nutramigen, Pregestimil, Alimentum, and Good Start. The first formula to be developed in this category dates back to the forties and answered special needs of very
sensitive babies that could not tolerate nor digest regular protein in
cow's milk or soya. To reduce the infant's exposure to whole protein, the cow's milk protein (casein or whey) is pre-digested in a test
tube and filtered down to a purified hydrolysate. Other ingredients
are easily absorbed and are often non-allergenic.

The casein-hydrolysate-containing formulas (Nutramigen, Preges-timil, Alimentum) are labeled "hypoallergenic" by the American Academy of Pediatrics and have been successfully used in cases of allergy and colic. Such highly processed and expensive formulas are recommended for infants that have a family history of allergy and have shown symptoms of allergies.

The whey-hydrolysate-containing formula (Good Start) is an accept-able alternative to cow's milk and soy protein formulas for infants who are intolerant but not allergic to cow's milk.

These formulas contain all the vitamins and minerals needed by the infant. They are also iron-fortified.

Evaporated whole milk formula

Evaporated milk is not recommended for newborn babies. The con-centration of protein, fat, and carbohydrate does not respect the in-fant's needs even when the evaporated milk is diluted and sweetened.

Nonetheless, if for economic reasons you cannot purchase a milk-based or soy-based infant formula, you may consider this type of milk as a third choice. On the positive side, compared with regular whole homogenized cow's milk, the protein has been heat-treated dur-ing the evaporation process and is more easily digested by the infant.

Before six months, dilute one part of evaporated milk with two parts of boiled water to decrease the protein and sodium content; sweeten with white sugar or dextrose to insure an adequate energy content. (Honey and corn syrup are not recommended before your baby is at least six months old.)

To obtain approximately 20 ozs. of formula:

- mix 7 ozs. of evaporated milk
- with 14 ozs. of cooled boiled water
- and 2 tablespoons of white sugar.

After six months, dilute one part of evaporated milk with one part of water.

Evaporated goat's milk

Goat's milk is sometimes considered the solution when the baby is intolerant of cow's milk. Few studies have shown the effectiveness of this strategy, but the belief is a thousand years old. While the nutri-tional content of goat's milk is quite similar to cow's milk, the pro-tein and fat compositions are slightly different. While whole pasturized goat's milk has a deficiency in folic acid and is not recommended as a suitable milk for the newborn, some canned evaporated goat's milk products (Meyenberg) are fortified with folic acid and vitamins D and C and may be considered adequate when diluted appropriately.

If you are considering using goat's milk for your baby, use the fortified evaporated form, and follow the same dilution directions as for the evaporated milk formula above to decrease the protein and sodium content.

Whole unmodified cow's milk

Whole milk is inappropriate for your infant for at least six to eight months after birth. The protein is excessive, hard to digest, causes gastrointestinal bleeding, and can lead to iron deficiency. The essential fatty acid content is very low, and the butterfat content is poorly absorbed. The carbohydrate content is too low. The minerals exceed the baby's needs and impose an additional burden on the immature renal system.

Whole cow's milk should not be introduced into your baby's diet until he eats 12 tablespoons of solid foods every day. The same restriction applies to whole unmodified goat's milk.

Partially or totally skim milk

These products are not appropriate for your infant during the first year of life. In the 70s, a growing number of babies started drinking skim or partially skim milk before six months. The pretext was to prevent atherosclerosis or obesity. Since then, researchers have verified the impact of such a practice on infants' growth and development. They have shown that babies on skim milk at four months drink larger amounts of milk and eat more solid foods to compensate for the decreased amount of calories. In spite of this, these babies gained weight less rapidly and lost an important amount of their fat tissues. These babies survived the crash diet but their ability to fight against infections or illness was questioned. Skim milk given too early triggers a survival mechanism that leads the baby into overeating food and milk in an attempt to be satisfied. This mechanism works against long-term weight maintenance and encourages the baby to gorge himself for satisfaction.

Skim milk, void of all essential fatty acids, does not support the development of the total nervous system. It also supplies excessive protein and minerals that can tax the baby's immature renal system.

Needless to say, the use of skim milk is strongly discouraged during the first and even the second year of life. The use of partially skim, 1 or 2 percent milk is also discouraged before 12 months.

Follow-up or weaning formulas

These formulas have been used in Europe for years and are now appearing on the U.S. market. They are adjusted to the baby's needs after six months and are iron-fortified. They offer no real advantage over breast milk, regular iron-fortified formula, or cow's milk once the baby is eating 12 tablespoons of solid foods each day. But they can be considered a valid option after six months.

The right milk at the right time

The appropriate milk at the right time is the key to infant health. Milk supplies all the needed nutrients during the first six months and then plays a major nutritional role until twelve months.

From birth to six months, to summarize, your choices are, in order of preference:

— breast milk;
— an iron-fortified infant formula;
— in special circumstances, an evaporated whole milk formula diluted and sweetened appropriately; an iron supplement is needed (see Chapter 8).

From six to twelve months, your choices are, in order of preference:

— breast milk;
— an iron-fortified infant formula;
— whole cow's milk once your baby is eating 12 tablespoons of solids;
— a follow-up or weaning formula.

After twelve months, you may use whole cow's milk, or introduce a partially skim milk to adjust to the rest of the family's habits. Totally skim milk is not recommended until two years of age unless there is a very special family problem.

The amount of formula to give your baby in 24 hours depends on the size, the age, and the activity of your baby. During the first weeks after birth, a baby is often hungry but swallows only small quantities of milk at each feeding. During the first week, your baby may request from six to 10 feedings daily. The second and third week, six to eight feedings may be enough.

As your baby reaches the first month, the interval between feedings increases and the volume of milk also increases; five to six feedings may suffice. From the third month on, four to five feedings will be enough. There is no maximum volume of milk to respect and no need to begin solids even if your baby demands more milk before six months.

Before changing formulas, make sure you have a good reason to do so. Many mothers interpret normal problems as symptoms of food allergy and try every formula on the market to solve the problem. This strategy is far from being guaranteed and sometimes can cause more harm than good.

If your baby is spitting up, it is not a sign of allergy. Spitting up small amounts of foods is a frequent problem in the first few months, due perhaps to the immaturity of the baby's digestive tract. To decrease the problem, avoid using an infant seat after feedings, and lay the baby on its stomach instead. Make sure your baby burps halfway through feedings. Avoid excitement or activities just after a feeding. If your baby is gaining normally, do not worry; if not, consult your doctor.

If your baby has colic with a milk-based or a soy-based infant formula, reexamine your feeding technique, avoid too much air swallowing, avoid under- or overfeeding; feed on demand; gently massage the abdomen. If all these suggestions remain without results, offer a protein-hydrolysate-type formula for at least two weeks and keep your fingers crossed until three months have passed.

The temperature of the formula will vary. Some babies prefer it warm in winter and cool in summer. If your baby prefers it warm, put the formula under hot, running water for a few minutes. Always check the temperature before you give it to your baby by testing a few drops on the back of your hand. If you use the microwave, be very careful. Shake the formula before using, and then make sure it is not too hot.

(See Chapter 12 for other possible problems.)

How to Prepare Infant Formula

It is recommended that you sterilize the infant's feeding equipment for the first four months.

1. Wash all equipment (bottles, nipples, caps, tongs, measuring cup, opener) and sterilize by boiling 5 minutes.

2. Boil for 10 minutes the water you will use to dilute the powder or the concentrate. Let it cool.

3. If you have any doubt concerning the safety of your local water supply, use sterile bottled water with a low mineral content.

4. Rinse top of can with boiling water; shake vigorously; open with a sterilized opener.

5. If using a ready-to-serve formula, pour it into the sterilized bottles.

6. If using the powdered form, pour cooled water into a large, sterilized pitcher; add proper amount of formula according to directions on the label. Gently stir.

7. If using the concentrate, pour cooled water into the bottles and add the proper amount of formula to each bottle.

8. Use the sterilized tongs to apply caps and nipples. Shake to mix the formula as needed.

9. Refrigerate immediately for use within 24 hours.

10. Once open, a can of ready-to-serve or concentrate should be emptied into a sterilized pitcher, covered, and refrigerated. Any unused portion should be discarded after 48 hours.

8
Vitamin and Mineral Supplements Before and After Six Months

In recent years, it has become an acceptable and widespread health routine to take extra vitamins and minerals. More than 50 percent of American adults swallow supplements every day. Very few among them have a precise idea of what they really need or what is really missing from their daily diet while many use these supplements in large doses to prevent illness or retard aging.

During the first years of life, the context is quite different. Supplements for babies are essentially considered to be nutritional complements. The role of these complements is to help the baby fill in nutritional gaps, not exceed nutritional needs.

A baby's body mass is relatively small, and excessive quantities of supplements can be more dangerous than for adults and present more risks later in life. Another forgotten fact is that under ideal conditions, an infant is born with nutrient stores accumulated during pregnancy and delivery. Fed by a well-nourished mother during nine months or so, having been granted a placental transfusion at birth prior to the cutting of the cord, the newborn has nutritional stores at her disposal: an underestimated reality.

If we look at the nutritional contribution of the various milks and solid foods given to infants before 12 months, we find very few possible or probable nutritional gaps. The need for vitamin and mineral supplements is therefore limited during the first year of life.

Depending on the milk you give your baby, possible missing nutrients include vitamin D and iron. Fluoride is not a missing nutrient but a supplement that is considered more a preventive measure. Vitamin B12 can be missing in the diet of a strict vegetarian infant, and a supplement becomes a necessity.

Vitamin D

Unlike any other vitamins, vitamin D is not present in significant amounts in foods except fish oils. It is naturally produced in the skin upon exposure to sunlight. It then helps the body absorb calcium and allows good bone growth.

When vitamin D is deficient, babies develop rickets, that is, have bowed legs and knock-knees that become visible when they begin to walk. Teeth are less well formed and decay earlier. Thirty years ago, rickets was not rare in northern parts of the U.S. Fortifying milk with vitamin D has since almost eliminated the problem. In recent years, only a few cases of rickets have been reported in the scientific literature. These cases were babies of dark or colored skin, breast fed by mothers on strict diets that did not include milk. The babies were not regularly exposed to sunshine.

The fact is that breast milk contains very little vitamin D, relatively inactive, even if you take a vitamin D supplement yourself. A breast-fed infant born during fall months with little exposure to sunlight needs a vitamin D supplement that provides 400 IU per day. Begin the supplement during the second week of life. Supplements available include:

- D-vi-sol infant drops, which supply vitamin D exclusively;
- Tri-vi-sol infant drops, which supply vitamins D, C, and A;
- Tri-vi-flor infant drops, which supply vitamins D, C, A, and fluoride.

Milk-based, soy-based, or protein-hydrolysate-based formulas are all fortified with adequate amounts of vitamin D. Evaporated whole milk is also fortified with an adequate amount of vitamin D. Babies fed such formulas do not need a vitamin D supplement.

Iron

Iron is part of the nutritional heritage that a baby receives at birth. This heritage depends on the mother's health and nutritional status and on the length of pregnancy. A term baby of normal weight who received a placental transfusion before the cord was cut usually has good iron stores for at least four months. A premature baby born at seven or eight months has generally used all his iron stores by the age of two months.

Iron accounts for 75 percent of the hemoglobin present in the body, and hemoglobin plays the crucial role of transporting oxygen to all body tissues.

Iron deficiency is the most frequent nutritional deficiency among U.S. infants before the age of two. It leads to mild anemia that can go unnoticed, and then to more severe symptoms of pallor, loss of appetite, decreased tolerance to exercise, irritability, decreased resistance to infection, and impaired behavior.

Breast milk contains little iron, but its iron is absorbed five times more efficiently than that in cow's milk or regular formula and ten times more efficiently than iron in iron-fortified formulas. Totally breast-fed, term infants do not need an iron supplement before six months. After six months, if they eat iron-fortified infant cereals on a daily basis, they get the needed iron.

Totally breast-fed, premature infants need an iron supplement in the form of ferrous sulfate by the age of two months at a dose of 1 mg per pound per day; never give more than 15 mg per day. Among iron supplements available are:

- Fer-in-sol iron drops;
- Tri-vi-flor infant drops with iron.

A baby fed an iron-fortified formula (milk-based, soy-based, or protein-hydrolysate-based) needs no iron supplement. One quart of such formula currently provides 12 mg of iron in the form of ferrous sulfate. In the past 20 years, the use of such iron-fortified formulas has doubled and has been credited for the declining incidence of anemia among babies.

A baby fed a regular infant formula (milk-based and not fortified with iron) requires an iron supplement by the fourth month. You may at this point give your baby an iron-fortified formula or an iron supplement in the form of ferrous sulfate.

A baby fed an evaporated whole cow's milk formula requires, by the fourth month, an iron supplement in the form of ferrous sulfate. Available supplements include:

- Fer-in-sol drops;
- Tri-vi-flor infant drops with iron.

The additional iron found in iron-fortified infant formulas or in the supplement of ferrous sulfate drops very seldom causes adverse reactions such as cramps, constipation, and gas. The only noticeable difference is in the color of the stools, which become dark brownish, greenish, or black.

Vitamin B12

Other vitamins and minerals are present in adequate quantities in breast milk and infant formulas under normal circumstances. However, vitamin B12 can become deficient in totally breast-fed infants of strict vegetarian mothers. A few tragic cases have been reported in the scientific literature where babies have suffered major neurological problems before the age of 12 months. Mothers had not eaten any animal foods, which supply vitamin B12, during their pregnancy and lactation. Breast milk had become deficient in this vitamin and could no longer support the infant's growth and development.

If you are a strict vegetarian, it is recommended that you take a vitamin B12 supplement during pregnancy and lactation. You should also give a vitamin B12 supplement to your baby, beginning in the second week of life. Liquid drops for infants containing several vitamins, including vitamin D and vitamin B12, are available on the market.

Fluoride

Fluoride given in appropriate quantities has been shown to decrease the incidence of dental caries by up to 50 percent. It acts before eruption of the teeth by improving the quality of the enamel. After eruption, it limits degradation of the enamel.

Breast milk has a very low fluoride content even if you take a supplement or even if you drink fluoridated water. Infant formulas are now prepared with defluoridated water, so their content is less than 3 parts per million.

If your local water supply is naturally or artificially fluoridated, your child will receive an effective dose to help her reduce tooth decay once she drinks a fair amount of water or of formula prepared with such water. If your water supply is not fluoridated, a supplement becomes a must. The most recent recommendation of the American Academy of Pediatrics issued in 1986 encourages fluoride supplementation for all babies, beginning the second week of life. Supplements available include:

- Karidium drops, of which 2 drops provide the daily recommended amount of 0.25 mg of fluoride;
- Tri-vi-flor infant drops.

Summing up supplements

Dietary supplements needed before six months depend essentially on the type of milk you give your baby. Accordingly:

The totally breast-fed baby born during spring months needs no supplement except for 0.25 mg of fluoride per day. If born during the fall months with little exposure to sunlight, the addition of 400 IU of vitamin D per day is recommended. If breast-fed by a strict vegetarian mother not supplemented herself with vitamin B12, the baby will also need 0.3 micrograms of vitamin B12. All supplementation should begin the second week of life.

A totally breast-fed, premature baby needs, in addition, an iron supplement in the form of ferrous sulfate by the age of two months: a dose of 1 mg per pound per day is recommended, and a limit of 15 mg per day has been set.

The formula-fed infant receiving an iron-fortified milk-based, soy-based, or protein-hydrolysate-based formula does not need any supplement if the formula is prepared with naturally or artificially fluoridated water. If such is not the case, the baby should receive 0.25 mg of fluoride per day, beginning the second week of life.

The baby fed a regular milk-based infant formula (non-fortified with iron) also requires an iron supplement in the form of ferrous sulfate by the fourth month.

The baby fed the evaporated whole milk formula requires an iron supplement in the form of ferrous sulfate by the fourth month. If the formula is prepared with water that does not contain natural or artificial fluoride, he also needs 0.25 mg of fluoride every day, beginning the second week.

After six months, the baby should start eating iron-fortified infant cereals and other sources of iron. Fruit and vegetables slowly increase the vitamin content of his diet. Milk remains his main source of nutrients.

If the local water is not naturally or artificially fluoridated, a fluoride supplement is recommended at a dose of 0.25 mg per day until the age of two.

Once your baby is taking approximately 12 tablespoons of solid foods every day and once he is drinking whole cow's milk, make sure he eats a variety of fruits and vegetables that are rich in vitamin C and other nutrients. No other supplements are recommended at this stage.

Excessive supplementation can happen in early years. Young children taking megadoses (large doses) of vitamins are at risk of developing toxic reactions. Many vitamins and minerals taken in large quantities can cause harm.

Although 400 IU of vitamin D is recommended to prevent rickets, excessive doses of vitamin D, levels of 1,400 IU, may actually retard growth.

Vitamin A in the form of retinol can cause serious problems such as confusion, leg pains, vomiting, and dehydration when taken in doses from 50,000 to 200,000 IU per day, compared with the recommended dose of 1,400 IU.

Beta-carotene, which is the vitamin A precursor, is much less toxic but can color the skin of some babies. They become slightly orange. The symptom is harmless and gradually disappears once the consumption of carrots or other vegetables rich in beta-carotene is decreased.

Iron taken in excess can cause toxic disorders in the liver. Iron supplements are the second source of drug poisoning among toddlers in the U.S.

Fluoride taken in excess can cause irreversible tooth mottling. Before you give a fluoride supplement to your baby, make sure your local water does not already contain fluoride, naturally or artificially.

9
Weaning

The whole weaning process implies getting your baby used to a different eating mode. It affects you and your baby, physically and emotionally. During the first year of life, weaning has a lot to do with leaving the breast, but it also means getting used to a bottle, learning to swallow solid foods, learning to drink from a cup. These changes are normal occurrences in the lives of all babies; however, any transition represents a challenge.

There is no unique rule, no perfect timing for all babies, but there is a certain logic that can help you decide the right moment for you and your baby to pass on to another eating experience.

Nutritionally speaking, in the case of a normal-weight, term baby, breast milk supplies all the needed nutrients for the first six months. After that age, breast milk no longer provides enough iron, and at around twelve months, it no longer fulfills the infant's protein needs. The contribution of other foods, therefore, becomes a must in the second half of the first year.

At six months, the baby has developed a different manner of using the tongue and mouth. He is ready to chew solid foods even though he has few or no teeth; the chewing exercise is even beneficial in the development of good teeth. If the baby is left on milk and purees for many more months, he becomes lazy and refuses texture for ages and ages. You've certainly heard of two-year-olds thriving on purees, unable to tackle real food!

Introducing a bottle

If you have chosen to breast-feed but plan an eventual return to work, or would simply like to enjoy a longer break between feedings once in a while, introduce an occasional bottle quite early to get your baby acquainted with it. Plan the "bottle exposure" after your milk supply is well established but before the baby reaches three months. If you wait three or four months, your baby may go on a bottle strike and make the transition quite painful.

Express your milk manually or with a pump, and offer it in a bottle. This helps maintain good milk production and allows your baby to feel at home with the taste of your milk. Choose a bottle nipple that closely resembles the natural nipple and breast during feeding.

Ask the father, the babysitter, or another person to give the bottle. To make things easier, leave the room during the feeding. Remember, in your arms or close to your odor your baby does not expect a bottle and might initially refuse it.

Supplementing breast milk

If you wish to supplement breast milk with an infant formula, make sure your milk production is already well established. Never forget that your supply responds to the baby's demand, and the more often you feed him, the more milk you produce. If you eliminate a feeding too soon, you worsen the potential problem of inadequate milk supply instead of helping it.

Here are a few general guidelines:

— If your baby is not gaining enough weight, begin by nursing him more often for two or three days before adding any supplementary feeding.

— If more frequent feedings do not work, offer the formula immediately after your baby has sucked from both breasts.

— If you are planning to alternate breast milk with infant formula before six months, always maintain the morning and the night feeding. Gradually replace one feeding at a time with a formula feeding. After your body has adjusted to this first substitution, replace a second feeding, thus slowly decreasing the lactation process. If you are not in a rush, the slower you do it the better, for you as well as for the baby.

If you need to stop breast-feeding suddenly, the lactation process will remain functional for more than a month, and your body will require time to adjust. Pumping your milk can help relieve some pain but will maintain the milk supply. It is better to space out milk expression sessions to decrease total milk production. At the beginning, you may experience considerable discomfort, including milk fever with chills and malaise. It is not a type of flu but a reaction of your system, which can last three to four days. You may feel depressed for both physiological and emotional reasons. Premature or unexpected weaning is not a failure, it is an accident.

When to wean

Who initiates the weaning process and when? In most cases, you initiate the weaning process for all kinds of reasons. This is natural and acceptable. Health professionals around the world encourage mothers to breast-feed for at least six months, but no one has set an upper limit. You are the best person to decide. You may wish to breast-feed for three months; congratulate yourself for this achievement. You may prolong it up to twelve months or beyond; that choice belongs to you. Every single day of breast-feeding is worth it.

Some babies initiate the weaning process, showing less and less interest in the breast. This can happen during the first year, at around four to five months, seven months, or nine to twelve months. If you wish to respond to your baby's message, you can plan a gradual and easy weaning.

Other babies suddenly refuse to nurse for various reasons: when your first menses occurs, when you've eaten foods that flavor the milk with an unpleasant taste, when you've changed your body odor with a new soap or a new perfume, when you are very tense, or when the baby is teething. There are remedies for such happenings, and you can counteract the "strike" by improving all aspects of the feeding strategy. But do not insist. If the baby's message persists, slowly introduce infant formula.

Introducing a cup

Introduction of a cup can be done quite easily. Some babies go from breast to cup at around seven to eight months without any problem. Once the baby has started solid foods, slowly introduce a cup with a special spout. After the noon meal or in the afternoon, offer milk in this cup. Babies enjoy the sound of their teeth on the rim of the cup, and they will swallow more and more liquid as days go by.

Once fruits are introduced in the menu, offer fruit juice in the cup. Babies learn very quickly to drink such a sweet-tasting beverage from a cup. I recommend that you dilute the juice with an equal volume of water, even if no sugar is added to the juice. The sweet taste of a fruit's juice can very quickly encourage overconsumption.

The prolonged use of the bottle well into the second or third year of life is not a sound practice. It can even give rise to severe dental caries when babies are given a bottle at bedtime.

The introduction of solid foods is a very important issue that requires a chapter-long discussion. It can easily be done without interrupting the breast-feeding routine.

10
Solid Foods: Slowly But Surely

Early in this century, babies waited for solid foods until twelve months. They were exclusively milk-fed and were often anemic. In the fifties, research teams started adding strained meat to infant formulas by age six weeks in order to prevent the lack of iron.

After many such trials and errors, experts in the field have come to the general conclusion that babies fed breast milk or iron-fortified formulas do not need any solid food before the age of four months. Some can even wait until six months without any risk. That is the recommendation of the Committee on Nutrition of the American Academy of Pediatrics.

You might have heard other stories and be confused because of the many different opinions about this particular issue. Some books still recommend solids at four weeks. Even doctors do not always follow the majority recommendation because they often give in to parental pressure. The message is yet to be unanimous, but the consensus has gained many adherents in the last twenty years. Before you give in to family or peer pressure, it is worth understanding the many reasons behind the four to six months recommendation.

The facts about solids

Solid foods cannot replace milk. Solids are not introduced in the baby's diet to replace milk but to complement it when milk alone can no longer provide all the essential nutrients. If solids are introduced too early, the baby's milk intake drops, yet the total nutritional content of his diet is not improved. Studies have compared the nutritional value of infant diets consisting of only milk with diets composed of milk and solids. The milk and solids diet did not provide additional nutritional value because the baby ate some solids and drank less milk. For the same amount of calories, solids provide less essential nutrients than milk.

To satisfy a hungrier baby before the age of four months, it is wiser to increase the number of milk feedings per day. The total volume of milk per day is not an issue at that age. Until five months or more, a baby needs at least four milk feedings a day. She can take forty ounces of milk per day and develop normally without solids.

Solid foods do not affect the baby's sleep. Many parents think that cereals given at bedtime promote a full night's sleep, but this solution is a dream not a reality. Recent research carried out in the Cleveland area showed that babies given cereals at five weeks did not sleep any longer than babies fed milk exclusively until four months. They observed that most babies slept six consecutive hours at around twelve weeks and slept eight consecutive hours at around twenty weeks, notwithstanding their food intake. Coming to a similar conclusion, a British study reports that 70 percent of infants sleep from midnight to 6:00 A.M. by three months of age, while 13 percent sleep through at around six months, and yet another 10 percent never sleep through, regardless of solid foods. Prolonged sleep reflects the baby's total neurological development and has very little to do with the food she eats, colic being one exception.

Solid foods need to be swallowed. Before the age of three to four months, a baby does not have a lot of saliva, and his tongue cannot push solid food toward the back of his mouth. He can suck very well, but the extrusion reflex inhibits normal swallowing. Feeding him solids at that stage is in fact force-feeding him. By sixteen to eighteen weeks, the extrusion reflex is gradually disappearing, and the baby has acquired neuromuscular coordination, which enables him to swallow solid foods.

Solid foods need to be digested and assimilated. At birth, the baby is able to digest breast milk or anything quite similar. He does not possess the complete array of digestive substances. He only has a fraction of the digestive enzymes needed to cope with a normal variety of foods. Before three months, he cannot properly digest cereals or other starches. Before six months, he cannot assimilate different fats. A baby who eats solids too early has great difficulty coping with certain substances and cannot totally assimilate them. A lot of undigested foods are found in his stools.

Solid foods impose an extra burden on the renal system. A newborn baby has immature kidneys that react very poorly to protein excesses. Foods such as undiluted whole cow's milk, meat, or egg yolk if given too early may cause serious problems in fragile babies.

Solid foods increase the risks of allergies. The baby's immune system is still quite vulnerable during the very early months. Normal production of antibodies gradually increases during the first year, peaking at around seven months of age. Once the baby has a larger army of antibodies at her disposal, once the mucosal barrier has matured, the risks of developing allergic reactions to food are diminished.

A slow introduction of solids at around six months is, therefore, especially beneficial for a baby whose family has a history of food allergies.

A slow introduction of solids respects the baby's needs. Before the age of four to six months, breast milk or infant formula provides all the nutrients a full-term baby needs. After that age, iron needs are not fully met. Protein, zinc, and energy needs also increase. Solid foods now begin to play a true nutritional role in the baby's diet.

At five or six months, a baby also has better control of her head and neck. She can express needs and wants, show hunger by moving the head forward, indicate how full she is by moving her head backward. These movements send distinct messages and allow you to respond to your baby's appetite. The harmony between your baby's need for solids and your feeding response can more easily be met by a slow introduction of solids at that age. This harmony fosters the development of good eating habits for a lifetime.

When to begin solids

The best time to start solid foods for your second baby may not be the same as with your first child. Although many agree on an ideal time for the introduction of solid foods, there is no standard timing for all babies. Each baby has its own calendar of growth and needs. Your baby's growth and general behavior are your best indicators. Signs such as the following can lead you to the final decision:

- a breast-fed baby requires more than 8 to 10 feedings per 24 hours, empties both breasts at each feeding, and always seems hungry;
- a formula-fed baby drinks at least 40 ounces per day, empties all bottles, and still seems hungry;
- your baby has doubled his birth weight and always looks hungry.

Just make sure your baby is crying for food and not for attention. Use solid foods as a last response to a cry after eliminating other causes of discomfort such as dirty diapers, uncomfortable position, need for light, need for water, or need for affection.

Do not delay the introduction of solid foods until nine months. At six months, a baby is able and ready to chew solid foods even though he has no teeth. If the introduction of solid foods is delayed until nine or ten months, the baby may resist and refuse foods having consistency and texture for years. For the same reason, introduction of textured foods is also a need at around six to seven months. Pureed foods are not to be served endlessly!

How to introduce solid foods

The first solid food to offer should be rich in iron. Many foods such as meats and liver contain large amounts of iron, but infant iron-fortified cereals are best suited as an introductory food. These specially prepared cereals supply an abundant quantity of iron and are easily digested and assimilated. The American Academy of Pediatrics recommends including such infant cereals on the baby's menu until two years of age. Regular whole-grain cereals and regular fortified dry cereals do not provide a comparable level of iron and cannot be as useful at this time.

Babies usually enjoy eating cereals and consume large quantities by the end of the first year.

Parents often neglect serving these cereals beyond twelve months, perhaps because of their consistency and taste. But by using such cereals as a flour substitute in pancake or muffin recipes, by mixing these cereals with fruit purees or yogurt, you can maintain a high iron content in your baby's diet during the second year of life.

Introduce cereals when your baby is somewhere between four and six months. Here's how to do it:

- begin with a single-grain cereal such as rice because it offers little risk of allergies;
- mix one teaspoon of infant dry cereal with breast milk or formula to obtain the consistency of a thick soup;
- serve with a small spoon after having breast-fed or given the formula; this strategy helps maintain an adequate milk intake and offers cereal as a plus;
- begin by serving the cereal at the morning meal after the milk feeding; after a few days, offer the same cereal at suppertime.
- always spoon-feed to provide chewing exercise and to prevent choking;
- after four or five consecutive days with the same cereal, introduce another single-grain cereal such as barley or oatmeal. If there is a family history of allergies, introduce wheat only after twelve months;

- never add sugar;
- once the single-grain cereals have been offered, introduce mixed grains;
- gradually increase the amount to a maximum of one-half cup of dry cereal per day by the end of the first year.

Choose plain cereals without added fruit because of their higher protein content and lower price. This will also make it easier to trace possible sources of food allergy.

Feeding Schedule Between Four and Five Months

(if your baby needs solid foods)

at dawn	breast milk or formula
breakfast	breast milk or formula infant cereal
lunch	breast milk or formula
supper	breast milk or formula infant cereal
evening	breast milk or formula
night time	breast milk or boiled water

The second solid food to introduce is vegetables. Two or three weeks after the cereals have been introduced, add pureed vegetables to the menu. Babies enjoy the flavor, especially if tasted before the sweet flavor of fruits. Vegetables bring along vitamins, minerals, and fiber with very few calories. They also bring color to the plate. Try these easy techniques:

- introduce one vegetable at a time; wait four to five days before you offer a new one;
- start with yellow vegetables: squash and carrots; follow with greens such as zucchini, asparagus, and green peas; then add broccoli and cauliflower;
- offer plain vegetables before mixed vegetables;
- always serve cooked vegetables at this stage, homemade purees or commercial baby food;

— always spoon feed;

— serve at the noon meal;

— start with one teaspoon the first day; gradually increase up to ten tablespoons by the end of the first year;

— never add salt, sugar, fat, or other seasonings;

— heat a small amount in a glass container in a double boiler or in the microwave; always stir and verify the temperature before you serve;

— discard any leftover food that has been in contact with the serving spoon and the baby's saliva.

The third solid food to introduce is fruit. Two or three weeks after vegetables have been added is a good time to introduce fruit. Fruits supply sweetness to the menu plus vitamins, minerals, and fiber. Here's how to proceed:

— offer one fruit at a time before mixtures of fruit;

— never add sugar, and wait until later to introduce spices;

— always spoon-feed;

— serve homemade purees or commercial baby food;

— offer cooked fruit except for bananas, papayas, and mangoes that can be fork-mashed or blended without cooking;

— avoid small fruit with seeds, such as strawberries, raspberries, and grapes until the child is well over two years of age; strained or pureed strawberries or raspberries can be given with other fruit or yogurt at the end of the first year;

— if there is a family history of allergies, avoid citrus fruit juices (lemon, orange, or grapefruit) or citric acid before twelve months;

— avoid commercial fruit desserts filled with sugar;

— offer fruit juices (apple, grape, prune) once the baby drinks from a cup. Dilute with an equal volume of boiled or bottled spring water to decrease the sweetness;

— two ounces of fortified apple juice usually provides all the vitamin C needed for one day;

— avoid fruit drinks or flavored fruit crystals.

Feeding Schedule Between Five and Six Months
(or beginning one month after the first solid food
has been introduced)

at dawn	breast milk or formula
breakfast	breast milk or formula
	infant cereal
lunch	breast milk or formula
	vegetable puree
supper	breast milk or formula
	infant cereal
	fruit puree
evening	breast milk or formula

The fourth solid foods to introduce should be rich in protein. Meat, poultry, fish, or substitutes such as tofu or pureed beans can gradually be introduced two to three weeks after the addition of fruit, once the baby is at least six months old. This food group provides high-quality protein, iron, zinc, more or less fat depending on the food, and calories. One serving a day is sufficient. Follow this pattern:

— start with white meat such as chicken, turkey, or fish;
— continue with beef, veal, liver, or lamb
— introduce mashed tofu, the silken type;
— avoid processed meats such as ham and bacon because of high sodium and nitrate content;
— choose fish that have less PCB residues such as small, farmed fish or ocean fish: sole, flounder, grouper, haddock, halibut, monkfish, salmon, or tuna:
— introduce one new meat every three to four days;
— offer homemade or commercial baby food;
— at first, serve only one teaspoon alone, not mixed with vegetables;
— offer this food group at the noon meal;
— never add salt or seasonings;
— gradually increase to a maximum of six tablespoons daily by the end of the first year;

- avoid seafood such as shrimps, lobster, clams, mussels, and scallops at that age because of the baby's vulnerability to allergy;
- if there is a family history of food allergy, delay the introduction of fish altogether until twelve months;
- never force your baby to eat!

Feeding Schedule Between Six and Nine Months

at dawn	breast milk or formula or whole cow's milk*
breakfast	infant cereal fruit puree cow's milk*, breast milk, or formula
lunch	pureed meat pureed vegetables fork-mashed fruit cow's milk*, breast milk, or formula
snack	finger foods (see page 89) water
supper	infant cereal vegetables or fruit cottage cheese or yogurt cow's milk*, breast milk, or formula
bedtime	cow's milk*, breast milk, or formula

*If your baby is eating 12 tablespoons of solid foods per day.

Introducing additional solids

Other foods are gradually introduced once cereal, vegetables, fruit, and protein are taken on a regular basis.

Egg yolk supplies protein, vitamins, and minerals but is no longer considered a good source of iron. It is not an essential food in the baby's diet but can be mixed into the noon meal a few times a week. Serve it as follows:

- hard boil and sift a small quantity into the vegetable or meat dish;

— start with one teaspoon a day and gradually increase to a maximum of two egg yolks per week;

— keep leftover yolk in the refrigerator for up to three days; use any leftover in salads and sandwiches for the rest of the family.

Yogurt supplies calcium, vitamins, protein, and lactic cultures in a very smooth-tasting package. It can be added to the menu once the baby is eating cereal, vegetables, fruit, and the protein group:

— start with plain yogurt made with whole milk;

— try homemade yogurt for a milder taste;

— avoid fruit-flavored yogurts and frozen yogurts loaded with sugar and very little fruit;

— once the baby is used to plain yogurt, add fruit purees or mashed bananas for extra flavor;

— 4 ozs. of yogurt can replace 4 ozs. of whole cow's milk

Fruit juices are quite easily accepted to say the least! Babies enjoy their sweet taste to the point where they want more and more juice and drink less and less milk. This shift affects the quality of the diet and the baby's health. Given in a bottle as a bedtime snack, juice provokes the development of dental caries. Given in large quantities, it can lead to chronic diarrhea. (See Chapter 13 on special problems.) Deal with juice as follows:

— introduce juice when fruits are already on the menu, and once the baby can drink from a cup;

— do not serve in a bottle;

— dilute with an equal part of water;

— serve at room temperature; do not heat;

— limit the daily intake to 4 ozs., knowing that 2 ozs. is enough to cover daily vitamin C needs;

— start with apple juice from organic apples or grape juice to limit the possibilities of allergies; follow up with orange or grapefruit juice, freshly squeezed or frozen and reconstituted, strained through a sieve;

— avoid fruit-flavored crystals that do not contain any fruit but loads of sugar, food colorings, and other additives.

Whole egg should not be introduced before the end of the first year, at least after ten months, because of the allergenic properties of the egg white. Once the baby's immune system is better developed, a poached, soft- or hard-boiled egg can be offered three to four times a week without any problem. Eggs are easily digested and can be eaten at suppertime surrounded by colorful vegetables. When the whole egg becomes part of the baby's menu, the egg yolk served alone has no more purpose and can be eliminated.

Foods to forget during the first year or so are foods that contain questionable ingredients such as large amounts of fat, sodium, sugar, food colorings, or additives:

- processed meats such as bacon, smoked sausages, commercial pates, smoked or cured meats, canned luncheon meats;
- puddings, cakes, sweet cookies, candies, chocolate, and jellos;
- fried foods and French fries;
- soft drinks because of the high sugar content;
- tea and coffee because of caffeine content;
- diet foods, including diet drinks sweetened with sugar substitutes; babies need the calories;
- foods prepared with fat substitute; babies need the essential fatty acids to develop normally.

Teething foods are always welcome for your baby, who needs to chew in-between meals during the prolonged teething period, from four to twenty-four months. Using the safe and sound teething foods, proceed as follows:

- offer a piece of Melba toast, dry whole-wheat toast cut in strips, or a bread crust;
- prepare small popsicles with water for a very soothing effect;
- offer a dentally approved teething ring; this can do a great job.
- avoid raw carrots and celery sticks to prevent choking during the first year; pre-cook the carrots a few minutes to make things safer;
- teething biscuits contain sugar and are not recommended.

(See finger foods during the transition period (Chapter 16).)

11
Commercial Baby Foods

Commercial baby foods have been on the market for over 80 years. Pre-cooked infant cereals were the first to be introduced, followed by canned fruit and vegetable purees. Canned, strained meats came in the 1930s. More recently, strained juices have made their appearance. Over 300 different products are now available in the United States.

The products of today are not the ones of yesterday. They have gone through major changes in their composition and presentation over the past 20 years:

- Small metal can containers were converted to glass containers in the early 1960s to decrease the lead content.
- MSG (monosodium glutamate), a flavor enhancer, was removed in 1969.
- Added salt was removed in 1977.
- Added sugar was reduced in the late seventies.
- Nitrite-cured meats (ham, bacon) have been replaced by nitrite-free cured meats in the seventies; pureed meats are heat-processed at a high temperature for a sufficient time to kill any trace of botulism-causing bacteria.
- Hydrogenated vegetable oils have recently been replaced with sunflower or soy oil.

Preservatives and artificial colors or flavorings are not presently used. For all of these reasons, commercial baby foods are safer today than they were 20 years ago.

As far as their nutritional content is concerned, a brief description of the existing products in each category allows us to draw some conclusions.

Dry Cereals

Infant dry cereals sold in powdered form include a large diversity of products.

1. The "classic" infant cereal is a refined cereal, enzyme-treated, and pre-cooked to gelatinize the starches. It is then fortified with iron, B vitamins, calcium, phosphorus, and polyunsaturated oils such as sunflower or soy oil. In this type of cereal, you find:

- single-grain cereals (rice, barley, and oatmeal) for beginners, with or without added fruit (Beech Nut, Gerber, Heinz);
- mixed-grain cereals, with or without added fruit (Beech Nut, Gerber, Heinz).

2. Organically grown whole-grain cereal is another type. This cereal is milled, then pre-cooked in water, drum-dried to a fine powder, and fortified with iron. Among this type, you find:

- single-grain cereal (brown rice, oatmeal) fortified with iron (Hearth's Best);
- mixed-grain cereals fortified with iron (Hearth's Best).

3. Natural whole-grain cereal with fruit is still another available product for babies. The whole-grain cereal is sprouted or ground and mixed with dried bananas and sometimes with amaranth (Health Valley).

The fortified, highly processed and refined cereals (type 1) are quite suitable for babies until 24 months and respect their nutritional need for iron.

The less processed, organically grown, whole-grain and iron-fortified cereals (type 2) are a better nutritional choice. This type of cereal provides the right amount of iron and at the same time more magnesium, more vitamin B6 because of less processing, and a small amount of fiber that can help many babies who become constipated at that age. It also contains less pesticide residues than type 1.

Type 3 cereals can be an alternative choice once single-grain cereals have been introduced, but they need to be completed with an iron drop supplement to meet the baby's important iron need until 24 months.

Vegetable purees

Vegetable purees for infants and babies are also available in many forms.

Single vegetable purees, called "beginners," "first foods," or stage 1, contain a single vegetable and water. The variety of vegetables offered in little jars is somewhat limited to yellow vegetables, green beans, beets, and peas (Beech Nut, Gerber, Heinz).

Some "single" vegetable purees are prepared from organically grown vegetables, but the variety is still quite limited (Hearth's Best, Simply Pure Foods).

The "mixed" vegetable purees contain the same basic vegetables plus potatoes, celery, or tomato paste to which is sometimes added a cereal flour, corn-modified starch, vegetable oil, or skim milk powder (Beech Nut, Gerber, Heinz).

Generally speaking, these commercial vegetable purees are suitable time savers. They provide vitamins and minerals, but don't forget that they have been heat-treated like any other canned vegetable. The only difference is the absence of added salt. Their overall nutritional content is good but does not quite compete with a homemade puree prepared at the last minute with the freshest ingredients or a frozen puree made using the proper methods (see Chapter 12). Their vitamin C content is not important because vegetables rich in vitamin C such as broccoli, cauliflower, and snow peas, are never offered in little jars.

Some "mixed vegetable purees" contain twice as many calories as the single vegetable purees because of the added ingredients. A baby over six months is better off with home-prepared, freshly cooked, fork-mashed vegetables served without added salt until the end of the first year.

Taste-wise, commercial vegetable purees will never be as delicious as homemade fresh or frozen purees. I know of no study on this issue, but I tend to think that babies given home-cooked zucchini, asparagus, or broccoli at a very tender age will enjoy the taste of such vegetables more readily than babies fed commercial carrots, beans, and sweet potatoes. I have met adults who prefer canned peas to fresh peas because of many years of exposure to the former.

Fruit purees and fruit

Fruit purees for babies are abundant on the market, from single fruit to fruit with cereals to fancy fruit desserts for babies.

"Single" fruit purees, called "beginners," "first foods," or stage 1, contain fruit, water, and 15 mg of added vitamin C, which represents 45 percent of the recommended amount for babies under 12 months (Heinz, Gerber, Beech Nut). Some also contain citric acid to reduce heating time and prevent oxidation.

A second group of "single" fruit purees contains tapioca and added sugar (Heinz, Gerber).

A third group of "single" fruit purees is prepared with organically grown fruit and water. Some contain the additional 15 mg of vitamin C (Hearth's Best), others do not (Simply Pure Foods).

"Mixed" fruit purees contain at least two different fruits, water, and 15 mg of added vitamin C. They may also contain fruit juice, flour, sugar, and yogurt (Beech Nut) or modified corn starch, modified tapioca, wheat flour, citric acid, vanilla, sugar, and corn syrup (Heinz and Gerber).

A second group of "mixed" fruit purees is prepared with organically grown fruit, water (Simply Pure Foods), and 15 mg of added vitamin C (Hearth's Best).

"Fruit with cereal" products are sometimes called "wet cereals" and represents another fruit option on the market. They contain water, fruit, high-fructose corn syrup or sugar, cereal, skim milk, and modified corn starch (Heinz, Gerber, Beech Nut).

"Fruit with cereals" supply the additional iron and B vitamins not because of the cereals themselves but because of the fortification. They could be useful for a baby who seldom eats dry infant cereals but remain a sweetened option with twice the amount of calories as single fruit purees.

"Fruit desserts" are the fanciest fruit options available. All contain sugar, modified corn starch, water, and fruits. Some even contain butter (Gerber, Heinz).

"Single" fruit purees with added vitamin C are, nutritionally speaking, quite suitable as first fruits for your baby. The ones without added sugar, citric acid, or tapioca are definitely a better choice. They can even be offered later on when you have no fresh fruit around.

"Mixed" fruit products provide some vitamin C because of fortification of the product, but with all of the added ingredients, they also supply twice as many calories as "single" fruit purees.

Overall, a baby over six months is much better off with homemade mixed fruit prepared without added sugar, starch, or cereal. Adding a small quantity of vitamin C-fortified apple juice increases the vitamin C content of the homemade fruit mixture. Other "fruit desserts" can be occasional treats but offer no nutritional advantage over homemade fruit mixtures.

Meat purees

Meat purees represent a smaller group of products. "Single" meats such as beef, veal, and chicken are prepared with broth and no other ingredient (Heinz, Gerber, Beech Nut). The nutritional contribution is valuable, and the product is sometimes easier for babies to swallow than homemade meat purees.

"Meat and vegetable" purees are mixtures of vegetables, modified corn starch, meat, and pastas or rice without any salt added. Liver, turkey, and lamb are offered in this series as well as processed meats such as ham and bacon.

With the exception of processed meats, which do not represent a wise nutritional choice even if nitrite-free, such meals can save time. Homemade mixtures of meat and vegetables are, however, a better nutritional choice.

Fruit juices

Strained fruit juices are the last but not the least of these commercial products for babies.

"Single" or "mixed" fruit juices are prepared from concentrates and offered with the addition of 40 mg of vitamin C, corresponding to 120 percent of the daily recommended amount for babies until 12 months (Heinz, Beech Nut).

Some "mixed" fruit juices also contain skim-milk yogurt (Gerber). Other "single" and "mixed" fruit juices are prepared with organically grown fruit. They contain juice, not a diluted concentrate, and are fortified with 15 mg of vitamin C, which represents 45 percent of the daily recommended amount for babies until 12 months.

Commercial juices supply good amounts of vitamin C, some potassium, and other vitamins. But fresh or reconstituted frozen juices, strained before serving, supply an equivalent amount of vitamins and minerals at a much lower cost. As mentioned in the previous chapter, fruit juices, even unsweetened, represent a sweet treat for babies used to drinking formula or milk. Some babies quite easily bypass milk for juices. It is, therefore, preferable to serve them juice diluted with an equal volume of water. Strained juices offered in single serving bottles can travel without refrigeration and are useful as an occasional snack outside the home.

In summary, if you decide to buy commercial baby foods, your best nutritional choice in each category is:

- among infant dry cereals: the organically grown, whole-grain and iron-fortified cereals;
- among vegetable purees: "single" vegetable, organically grown or regular;
- among fruit purees: "single" fruit, organically grown or regular with no other added ingredients than water and vitamin C;

— among meat purees: "single" meats prepared with broth only.

The cost of commercial baby foods is about twice the cost of home-made baby foods. Even greater savings can be made when fresh fruit and vegetables are in season. If you decide to prepare your own baby food or to alternate between commercial and homemade, consult the next chapter.

12
Homemade Baby Foods

More mothers, including working mothers, are preparing homemade purees for their babies. Some alternate between homemade and commercial baby food but all want to provide the best nutritional value. Some fill up the freezer for a long-term supply, but there is no need to prepare large quantities of these "first" purees. Once your baby has tasted most of the proposed purees, she soon will be ready for fork-mashed, more consistent foods.

Time is a limiting factor, but the proposed blender-freezer method is an easy one to follow. It eliminates last-minute preparation. If you prefer to cook smaller quantities just before mealtime, follow the same guidelines concerning the choice of foods and the sanitation but forget about the cooling, the freezing, and the reheating steps.

Quality, variety, and nutritional value are the key words.

Homemade vegetable purees do not only include yellow vegetables; they allow you to introduce broccoli and cauliflower purees, which are rich in vitamin C and folic acid. Beautiful vegetables such as zucchini and asparagus are also easy to prepare. Organically grown produce is another option when available.

Fruit purees are quite easy to prepare. Add variety and taste with fresh-strained mango or fork-mashed papaya.

Poultry purees are simpler to prepare than ever with boneless, skinless, grain-fed chicken breasts.

Fish purees bring easily digested protein along with some omega-3 fatty acids.

The economic benefits of homemade purees are important, the price coming to about half the cost of commercial products, all groups of foods included. The best savings are made when fresh fruit and vegetables are in season, the cost then going down to less than one-third of the commercial price.

Natural flavor is another asset of homemade purees. Because of limited heat treatment, the taste comes closer to the original flavor and varies according to the season. Babies enjoy homemade purees. Over the years, I have heard of only one or two babies who actually preferred the commercial taste.

The advantages of homemade purees are irrefutable, but the overall quality remains under your control!

The rules of the game

Homemade purees can compete with commercial baby food if you follow simple but important guidelines. Make sure your baby food is safe and nutritious.

Choose first-quality ingredients. The final quality of homemade purees depends on the quality of the ingredients you use to prepare them. This applies to all recipes but is especially important when it comes to baby food.

Firm but ripe fresh fruit and fresh vegetables when in season are your best choices. When fresh fruit and vegetables are not good looking, not available, or too expensive, unsweetened frozen fruit and unsalted frozen vegetables, with no sauce or other flavorings, are suitable alternatives.

To reduce the presence of pesticides in your baby's menu, buy certified organic fruit and vegetables. Babies are more sensitive to environmental contaminants and pesticides because of their small body size. They take in more food per pounds of body weight than adults and more contaminants per pound also. If organic products are not available or too expensive, wash fruits and vegetables thoroughly and peel before cooking.

Canned fruit and vegetables are not appropriate. Even if some canned fruit and vegetables are available without added salt or sugar, they have been heat-treated and have lost some vitamin and mineral value. The whole idea of making your own baby food is to obtain a more nutritional product, not the opposite.

Fresh or frozen meats, lean parts in particular, fresh or frozen poultry, organic or regular, are all suitable choices. Processed meats of all kinds are not acceptable.

Fresh or frozen fish is a valid choice. For less PCBs and other residues, choose farmed or ocean fish, the smaller the better. Canned fish contains too much sodium and is not recommended before 12 months.

Follow a few hygienic rules. To eliminate the possibility of food contamination and to protect your baby from unnecessary infections, simple measures are to be taken:

- wash your hands before handling any food that will be used to prepare the baby food;
- use utensils, containers, and cookware that are impeccably clean;
- once the food is cooked and blended, cover and refrigerate immediately. Never let cooked food sit at room temperature;

— when you prepare small quantities of food to be
eaten immediately, do not keep the food more
than three days in the refrigerator;

— do not refreeze a thawed puree.

Assemble the needed utensils. Since homemade purees are introduced between the ages of four to six months, very smooth purees without lumps are required for only a few months at the most. By the time your baby has reached seven to eight months, she can chew more easily and be served food mashed with a fork.

A blender or a food processor makes your job much easier, but you can manage with an inexpensive manual food mill or a coffee grinder to prepare smaller quantities.

You also need: pots and pans, measuring cups and measuring spoons, individual ice-cube containers, freezer bags with ties (capacity of 1 pint and 1 quart), labels, and small aluminum plates.

Cook rapidly. Well-cooked foods are easier to digest while overcooked foods lose many vitamins and minerals.

Vegetables can be steamed or cooked in the microwave. Both methods use very little water and require very short cooking times. Both methods have been shown to minimize nutrient losses. Frozen vegetables should not be thawed before cooking and should be cooked rapidly.

Meat, fish, and poultry are cooked in small amounts of liquid.

Fruit is peeled and poached a few minutes in a small amount of water or fruit juice. This can be done on top of the stove or in the microwave. Ripe bananas, papayas, or mangoes can simply be mashed with a fork or pureed in the blender and served without any cooking.

Process no more than one and one-half to two cups of food at one time. Reduce this quantity to one cup in the case of poultry or meat. Large quantities of food hamper the blender's operational capacity and affect the quality of the final product.

Do not add any salt or sugar. Babies do not need any seasonings during the first year of life. They enjoy the real flavor of vegetables without added salt and will never refuse apples, pears, bananas, or other fruit *au naturel.*

The addition of salt during these early months may overload the baby's renal system (kidneys) while the addition of sugar cultivates the need for sweets. Even honey is not recommended before 12 months because of potential problems with botulinum spores.

To avoid such additions, never add salt to the cooking water and never season the foods before reducing them to a puree. If you want to serve some of the same foods to the rest of the family, add salt or seasonings once you have set aside the food for the baby.

Pour into ice-cube trays and cool. Once the puree is completed, pour it into ice-cube containers. Each cube used for the following recipes contains two ounces of food. Cool the puree in the refrigerator before freezing. If you only prepare a small quantity of food, you can store the puree in a covered container in the refrigerator for two or three days.

Cover the ice-cube containers with a sheet of wax paper and place in the coldest part of the freezer, far from the door. Allow 8 to 12 hours for complete freezing to take place.

Place frozen purees in plastic bags. Once the purees are frozen, remove the ice-cube trays form the freezer and empty the cubes into small freezer bags, one type of food per bag. Seal the bag by withdrawing the air with a straw. Label each bag with the type of food and the date. Quickly return the bags to the freezer.

Purees can be kept this way in the freezer for varying lengths of time depending on the ingredients:

vegetables	6 to 8 months
fruits	6 to 8 months
cooked meat and poultry	10 weeks
cooked fish	10 weeks
vegetables and meat meal	10 weeks
purees made with milk	4 to 6 weeks

Reheat in a double boiler or in the microwave. At mealtime, remove the number of cubes needed from the freezer bags, and put them in a glass container or a glass bowl. Warm up the cubes for a few minutes in a double boiler or for 30 seconds in the microwave. Avoid overheating. Always stir the food with a spoon to distribute the heat. Before serving, always verify the temperature by putting a drop of food on your wrist.

VEGETABLES

Puree of Asparagus

A spring delicacy.

Ingredients

1 lb. tender, young asparagus in season
water

Preparation

Snap off tough ends and discard. Wash tips and tender stalks. Cut in 2-inch pieces. Steam asparagus over boiling water approximately 10–15 minutes or until tender.

In the microwave, place asparagus pieces in a covered glass dish with ¼ cup of water. Cook at high power 6–9 minutes. Stir with a fork after half the cooking time.

Remove from heat and cool slightly.

Place half the asparagus in the blender with a small amount of water. Puree. Repeat with the remaining asparagus.

Pour into ice-cube trays and freeze.

Yield: 1 ice-cube tray full

Storage life: 6 months

Puree of Beets

Serve with a bib on you and another on the baby. Wait until your baby is eight months old because of high nitrate content. The same restriction applies to spinach.

Ingredients

1 lb. young beets
water

Preparation

Scrub beets. Cut off all but 2 in. of the tops. Do not peel. Leave whole. Steam 30–40 minutes in pressure cooker. Or microwave beets in covered glass dish with 2 tablespoons of water at high power for 12 minutes or until tender.

Cool slightly. Peel and slice cooked beets. Place in the blender with ¼ – ⅓ cup of fresh water. Puree. Pour into ice-cube trays and freeze.

Yield: 1 ice-cube tray full

Storage life: 6 months

Puree of Broccoli

Bright green broccoli has a sweet and pleasant flavor. It is rich in vitamins C and A, iron, calcium, and folic acid.

Ingredients

1 bunch fresh broccoli (approx 1 ½ lbs.)
water

Preparation

Cut off and discard the stalks. Keep only the flower part for the puree. (Use the stalks for soups or stir fries for the rest of the family.) Steam the broccoli over boiling water 10–15 minutes until broccoli is tender but still very green.

In the microwave, place broccoli in a covered glass dish with 2 tablespoons of water. Cook at high power 7–10 minutes. Stir with fork halfway through cooking time.

Remove from heat and cool slightly.

Place half the broccoli with ¼ cup of water into the blender. Puree. Repeat with the remaining broccoli.

Pour into ice-cube trays and freeze.

Yield: 1 ice-cube tray full

Storage life: 6 months

Puree of Carrots

Babies love the color and the flavor of carrots. Choose organic carrots when possible to reduce the nitrate content.

Ingredients

2 lbs. fresh carrots
water

Preparation

Remove tops. Wash. Scrape, peel, and scrub well with a stiff brush. Cut into 1-in. pieces. Steam carrots over boiling water 15–20 minutes or until tender.

In the microwave, place prepared carrots in covered glass dish with 1–2 tablespoons of water. Cook at high power 15–18 minutes. Stir with fork after half the cooking time.

Allow to stand 3 minutes before pouring into the blender.

Place 1 ½ cups of cooked carrots and ⅓ cup of fresh water into the blender. Puree. Repeat with the remaining carrots.

Pour into ice-cube trays.

Yield: 2 ice-cube trays full

Storage life: 6 months

Puree of Cauliflower

Cauliflower, as a member of the cabbage family,
is very rich in vitamin C.

Ingredients

1 small head of cauliflower
water
½ cup whole milk or soy milk

Preparation

Separate into small florets. Remove any green
stalks. Wash well. Steam over boiling water 15–20
minutes or until tender.

In the microwave, cook florets in a covered glass
dish at high power 9–11 minutes. Stir with a fork
after half of the cooking time.

Allow to stand 3 minutes before putting into
blender.

Place in blender, 1½ cups of florets with 1 cup
of water and ¼ cup of whole or soy milk. Puree.
Repeat with the remaining ingredients.

Pour into ice-cube trays and freeze.

Yield: 2 ice-cube trays full
or less, depending on
the size of the
cauliflower

Storage life: 4 to 6 weeks

Puree of Green Beans

The younger the green beans, the better the puree. Frozen green beans can also be used.

Ingredients

1½ lbs. tender, fresh green beans
water

Preparation

Wash and snap off ends. Cut beans into thirds. Steam over boiling water approximately 10–15 minutes or until tender.

In the microwave, place beans in a covered glass dish with ¼ cup of water. Cook at high power 15–19 minutes. Stir with a fork after half of the cooking time.

Allow to stand 3 minutes before putting into the blender.

Place half the cooked beans and ⅓ cup of water in the blender. Puree. Repeat with the remaining beans.

Pour into ice-cube trays and freeze.

Yield: 2 ice-cube trays full

Storage life: 6 months

Puree of Green Peas

Very green, very rich in iron, and quite sweet!

Ingredients

2 cups fresh green peas (2 lbs. unshelled)
water

Preparation

Shell and wash just before cooking. Steam peas over boiling water 12–15 minutes or until tender.

In the microwave, place peas in a covered glass dish with ¼ cup of water. Cook at high power 8–11 minutes. Stir with fork after half of the cooking time. Allow to stand 3 minutes.

Pour into the blender with ¼ cup of water. Puree. Pour into ice-cube trays and freeze.

Yield: 1 ice-cube tray full

Storage life: 6 months

Puree of Winter Squash

Winter squash and pumpkin are filled with
vitamin A.

Ingredients

1 winter squash (acorn, butternut)
water

Preparation

Wash. Bake squash whole in a 350°F. oven for
about 1½ hours.

In the microwave, cut squash in half and remove
seeds. Place cut side down in a shallow glass dish.
Cover. Cook at high power 12–16 minutes or until
tender.

Let stand 3 minutes.

Place the flesh in the blender with ¼ cup of water.
Puree.

Pour into ice-cube trays and freeze.

Yield:	1 ice-cube tray full or more, depending on the size of the squash
Storage life:	6 months

Puree of Zucchini

Zucchini has a sweet and soft flavor. The puree is a pretty spring green. Babies enjoy!

Ingredients

1 ½ lbs. small zucchinis
(7 to 8 small ones)
water

Preparation

Wash, scrub lightly, but do not peel. Remove stem and blossom ends. Cut into ½-in. slices. Steam zucchini 10–12 minutes or until tender.

In the microwave, place zucchini in a covered glass dish. Cook at high power 11–13 minutes. Rotate dish after half of the cooking time.

Allow to stand 3 minutes.

Place half the cooked zucchini in the blender without adding any water. Puree. Repeat with the remaining zucchini.

Pour into ice-cube trays and freeze.

Yield: 2 ice-cube trays full

Storage life: 6 months

FRUIT

Apple Sauce

Organic apples are a wise choice if you cook the apples with the skin. Cooking time varies according to type of apples used. Ripe McIntosh apples in season produce a soft pink and sweet puree. Once your baby is 12 months or older, modify this classic recipe by adding cinnamon for extra taste.

Ingredients

8 to 10 apples
water

Preparation

Scrub and wash the apples well. Do not peel. Remove cores, cut into quarters, and slice. Place apples in a saucepan with ½ cup of water. Bring to a boil, reduce heat, and simmer for about 20 minutes or until tender.

In the microwave, place apples in a covered glass dish with ½ cup of water. Cook at high power for 12–15 minutes or until tender.

Allow to stand 5 minutes to cool.

Place 2 cups of cooked apples in the blender and puree until the peel has completely disappeared. If the blender is not powerful enough to pulverize all the peel, pass the puree through a sieve or peel the apples before cooking. Repeat the same operation with the remaining apples.

Pour into ice-cube trays and freeze.

Yield: 2 ice-cube trays full

Storage life: 6 months

Puree of Pear

Different pears provide different flavors. You may wish to prepare half the recipe with bosc or French pears and the other half with red Anjou pears. When your baby has been introduced to all fruit, cook the pears in apple juice or prepare a pear-and-apple puree by using both fruits in the same puree. This can be fork-mashed later on.

Ingredients

9 to 11 fresh, medium pears
½ cup of water

Preparation

Peel pears, quarter, and core. Place into a saucepan with ½ cup of water. Simmer for 20–30 minutes or until pears are tender.

In the microwave, place pears in a covered glass dish with ½ cup of water. Cook at medium power 10–15 minutes.

Allow to stand at least 5 minutes before pouring into the blender.

Place half the cooked pears in the blender with 2 tablespoons of the cooking water. Puree. Repeat with the remaining pears.

Pour puree into ice-cube trays and freeze.

Yield: 2 ice-cube trays full

Storage life: 6 months

Puree of Peach

Fresh peaches are a seasonal luxury. Nectarines are easier to find and may replace peaches when out of season. Simply fork-mash when your baby is more than eight months old.

Ingredients

4 cups fresh peaches, peeled, pitted, and sliced
⅓ to ½ cup water

Preparation

Put peaches and water into a saucepan. Bring to a boil, reduce heat, and simmer gently for about 15–20 minutes or until peaches are tender.

In the microwave, put peaches in a covered glass dish with ½ cup of water. Cook at medium power for 7–8 minutes or until tender.

Allow to stand 5 minutes before processing in the blender.

Place 2 cups of cooked peaches in the blender with 1 tablespoon of cooking water. Puree. Repeat with the remaining peaches.

Pour into ice-cube trays and freeze.

Yield: 2 ice-cube trays full

Storage life: 6 months

Puree of Apricots

Apricots are a good source of vitamin A but are very seasonal. If you are lucky, you will be able to offer this special puree to your baby.

Ingredients

4 cups fresh, ripe apricots
½ cup water

Preparation

Wash very well. Do not peel. Pit and slice the apricots. Place fruit into a saucepan, bring to a boil, reduce heat, and simmer for about 15 minutes, until apricots are tender.

In the microwave, place fruit in covered glass dish with ½ cup of water. Cook at medium power for 8 minutes or until the fruit is tender.

Allow to stand 5 minutes.

Place half the cooked apricots in the blender with ¼ cup of cooking water. Puree. Repeat with the remaining apricots.

Pour into ice-cube trays and freeze.

Yield: 2 ice-cube trays full

Storage life: 6 months

Puree of Prunes

Prunes are quite sweet, rich in iron, and rich in fiber. A sure favorite! Once the baby has been introduced to all fruit, mix an equal share of this puree with applesauce for a different treat.

Ingredients

1 ½ cups pitted prunes (12-oz. bag)
2 cups hot water
1 cup cold water

Preparation

Soak prunes in hot water for 5–15 minutes; drain. Place the prunes and cold water in a saucepan; bring to a boil; reduce heat and simmer for about 20 minutes. Remove from heat and cool slightly.

Place half the prunes with ⅓ cup of cooking liquid in the blender. Puree. Repeat with remaining fruit. Pour into ice-cube trays and freeze.

Yield: 1 ice-cube tray full

Storage life: 6 months

MEAT, FISH, AND POULTRY

Puree of Beef

The same directions can be used to prepare a puree of veal.

Ingredients

1 lb. lean, tender beef, cut in 1-in. cubes
1 stalk of celery, chopped
3 carrots, peeled and cut in pieces
2 medium potatoes, peeled and quartered
1 tablespoon minced onion

Preparation

Place beef and 2¼ cups of water into a saucepan; simmer for about 45 minutes. Add celery, carrots, and potatoes; cook another 35 minutes or until tender. Remove from heat and cool slightly.

Separate the beef from the vegetables. Place ¾ cup of cooked meat in the blender with ⅓ cup of cooking water. Puree until nice and smooth. Repeat with remaining beef.

Pour into ice-cube trays and freeze.

Yield: 10–12 cubes

Storage life: 10–12 weeks

Tip: Puree the cooked, discarded vegetables with extra broth and serve as a garden soup to the rest of the family.

Puree of Chicken

Use turkey breast for variety and economy, depending on the market specials. Organic chicken is also a recommended product.

Ingredients

2 boneless, skinned chicken breasts
water or unsalted vegetable broth

Preparation

Place the chicken breasts in a steamer. Steam over boiling water 15 minutes or until the chicken flesh is cooked. Remove and cut up the chicken into big pieces.

Place ½ cup of chicken meat with ⅓ cup of broth in the blender. Puree until nice and smooth. Repeat with remaining chicken.

Pour puree into ice-cube trays and freeze.

Yield: 1 ice-cube tray full

Storage life: 10–12 weeks

Puree of Chicken Livers

Liver is a very rich source of iron, and chicken livers have a softer texture and flavor than others.

Ingredients

5 to 6 chicken livers (from organic chickens)
homemade chicken broth, unsalted
or
vegetable broth

Preparation

Cut livers in half and remove the white membrane. Place in a saucepan with 1 cup of broth. Simmer gently for 10 minutes or until livers are a gray-brown inside. Remove from heat and cool slightly.

Place a few chicken livers in the blender with a small amount of cooking liquid. Puree until smooth. Repeat with remaining liver.

Pour into ice-cube trays and freeze.

Yield: 6 cubes

Storage life: 10–12 weeks

Puree of Fish

Babies enjoy the taste and texture of fish.
Mothers enjoy the short preparation involved!
Fish is an excellent source of protein and of
omega-3 fatty acids.

Ingredients

½ lb. fish fillets (ocean or farmed fish)
(sole, flounder, halibut, haddock, salmon)
½ cup whole milk (do not use 2% or skim milk
until the baby is 1 year old)

Preparation

Pour ¼ cup of milk into a pan and gently heat. Add
the fish fillets. Cover and poach over low heat 5–10
minutes or until the fish flakes easily with a fork.
Remove from heat and cool slightly.

Place half the cooked fish and cooking milk into
the blender. Blend until smooth. Add more milk if
needed. Repeat with the remaining fish.

Pour into ice-cube trays and freeze.

Yield: 8 cubes

Storage life: 4–6 weeks

Tip: Once your baby has been introduced to all basic
foods, add 2 tablespoons of minced onion during
poaching for extra flavor.

13
Questions and Problems

Questions relating to feeding are quite frequent during the early months after birth while worries concerning eating behavior become more important in the second part of the first year of life. Questions concerning obesity or cholesterol are also on your mind when thinking of the future. This chapter deals with these issues and provides answers that will help you better manage such challenges.

What to do about spitting up

Spitting up, or regurgitation, is a fairly common problem during the first months of life. It is quite different from vomiting and can be described as spitting up small amounts of food that dribble from the mouth during and after a meal. If is caused by the immaturity of the digestive tract and should not be interpreted as an allergic reaction. It does not affect your baby's growth nor his appetite and slowly disappears by the third month of life.

You can nevertheless minimize the problem by trying the following strategies:

- Lay your baby on its stomach after each feeding instead of putting him in an infant seat; the use of infant reclining seats, also called Chalasia chairs, has been shown to cause such problems.
- Avoid overfeeding your baby by responding to his cues of fullness or satiety.
- Make sure your baby is never left alone to feed with a propped bottle.
- Avoid playing with or exciting your baby just after a feeding.
- Make sure your baby burps at least once during a feeding.

Vomiting is another problem altogether. It is a forceful expulsion of large quantities of food or milk. It is usually associated with another illness such as fever or a gastrointestinal infection and requires medical attention.

How to handle colic

Colic is a manifestation of acute pain that usually begins during the third or fourth week of life and gradually disappears by the fourth month of age. It is seen as often in breast-fed infants as among formula-fed babies.

You think your baby has colic. She cries, even screams for hours, usually in late afternoon or early evening. Her abdomen is hard and distended and she finds no comfort even in your arms. There are many possible causes of infantile colic, from under- to overfeeding, poor burping technique, food intolerance, air swallowing, or a greater need for affection.

If you are breast-feeding:

- Do not hesitate to feed on demand to satisfy your baby's frequent needs for food, but make sure you empty the first breast before offering the second; short feedings on each breast provide too much lactose and not enough milk fat, which in turn causes hunger, colic, and crying.
- Look over your feeding position and make sure your baby does not swallow too much air.
- Try eliminating from your diet all milk products for five to ten days (see Chapter 6 for a balanced menu without milk products). If you see some results but still witness sessions of pain, try eliminating other proteins such as beef or chicken or soy. Plan your menus around protein-rich foods that you did not eat frequently during your pregnancy. See how it works. If you see no results after five to ten days of elimination, resume your usual diet and look for another solution.

If you are formula-feeding:

- Try a protein-hydrolysate-based formula (see Chapter 7) for a few weeks; if the problem is relieved, continue on with such a formula until the fourth month.
- Massage your baby's abdomen and take her in your arms more often.

Never forget that colic is a temporary problem. If it lasts beyond four months, it may require special medical investigation.

What to do when baby has diarrhea

It is important first to define diarrhea and distinguish between loose stools and severe diarrhea.

Before 12 months: **Mild diarrhea** in a formula-fed baby manifests itself by chronic loose stools and can be caused by a food intolerance. After solids have been introduced, diarrhea can occur as a sudden change in the consistency of the stools caused by some unusual food in your baby's diet. Both cases are considered a minor health problem.

Semi-liquid stools are not always considered a problem. Healthy, breast-fed babies can normally pass eight to ten stools a day during the first weeks of life. These stools are often loose, yellow, brown, or dark green in color. This is not a case of diarrhea. As weeks go by, bowel movements become less frequent, but the consistency remains soft when breast milk is the only food.

Chronic semi-liquid stools in a formula-fed baby are less frequent. The problem can be considered diarrhea and may be caused by an intolerance to milk protein or to lactose. A change to a soy-based, lactose-free formula may alleviate the problem, or if your family has a history of food allergy, a protein-hydrolysate-based formula may be a better choice.

After 12 months: After a variety of solids have been introduced, mild diarrhea may be caused by overconsumption of fruit juice. Decreasing the use of juice and increasing the consumption of whole milk may solve the problem.

Before or after 12 months: **Severe diarrhea** is also called gastroenteritis; it is caused by a viral infection. Its manifestations include watery stools often accompanied by vomiting and fever. It is considered a serious health problem and requires immediate action to prevent dehydration, which causes 500 deaths and 200,000 hospitalizations per year among young children in the U.S., according to the Centers for Disease Control.

To replace water losses and minerals in the baby's body, give her plenty of fluids in the form of an "oral electrolyte solution" found in grocery or drug stores: Lytren, Pedialyte, Rehydralyte, or Resol. These drinks have the right amounts of water, salts, and sugar while juices, sodas, or soft drinks do not contain the right amounts, may worsen the situation, and may retard recovery.

> — Offer ½ cup of the "oral electrolyte fluid" every hour, using a bottle or small spoon.
> — Call your doctor or the public health clinic.

— Continue breast-feeding or formula-feeding your baby as often as possible. If your baby is already eating solid foods, continue feeding them; infant cereals, bananas, and cooked meats are good foods to include in her menu. Even if the appearance of the stools has not improved, this procedure reduces weight loss, shortens the duration of the diarrhea, and helps your baby recover faster.

— If your baby vomits, continue giving the oral electrolyte solution, one teaspoon every two to three minutes, until vomiting stops.

— A baby under 12 months may require as much as one quart of the oral electrolyte solution during an acute attack of diarrhea.

— To prevent further contamination, carefully wash your hands with soap and water after changing your baby's diaper and before preparing food.

How to prevent or cure constipation

Constipation is defined as a problem of consistency, that is, the elimination of dry and hard stools. It can become so painful that some babies may withhold their stools.

Breast-fed babies are seldom constipated while formula-fed babies may have harder stools.

Constipation occurs more often when solid foods are first introduced and when whole cow's milk replaces breast milk or the formula. Here are some measures you can take to overcome the problem.

Before six months:

— increase your baby's fluid intake by giving boiled or sterilized water in-between feedings;

— if your baby is in pain at every stool and has dry, hard stools, use two to three teaspoons of mineral oil per day, 1 teaspoon per feeding. Do not use for more than a month without consulting your doctor;

— if the problem persists, a medical examination should be performed to eliminate the possibility of an anal fissure.

Between six and 12 months:

- increase your baby's water intake between feedings;
- introduce a whole-grain infant cereal instead of the refined types (See Chapter 11.);
- if the first two suggestions do not bring any improvement, mix one tablespoon of natural wheat bran with the infant cereal mixture; this small quantity of bran does not interfere with the baby's total calorie intake or mineral absorption.
- instead of wheat bran, you can add one teaspoon of cold-pressed linseed oil to the cereal.

After 12 months:

- serve grated, raw vegetables and pieces or raw fruit on a daily basis;
- offer water between meals;
- serve fiber-rich, whole-grain products such as brown rice, whole-wheat bread, and whole-wheat pasta instead of white rice, white bread, and white pasta;
- limit cow's milk intake to a maximum of 32 ounces a day;
- mix one to two tablespoons of natural wheat bran with the infant cereal or with yogurt; this small quantity of bran does not interfere with the baby's total calorie intake or mineral absorption;
- add one teaspoon of cold-pressed linseed oil to the infant cereal.

When your baby has a tendency to be constipated, he requires a regular routine to function properly. Allow sufficient time for toilet training after your child has reached 18 months, which will favor normal elimination.

How to respond to food refusal

Never force your baby to eat, never! This advice is valid for all ages under all circumstances.

Babies are hungry some days, less hungry other days. Appetite normally slows down when growth slows down at the end of the first year, and hunger strikes can happen any day.

Your response can enhance the development of a happy eating relationship or do the opposite. A relaxed attitude is your surest strategy from the time of birth on, but it is also the most difficult one to manage.

To reduce your anxiety, always offer the most nutritious foods but allow your child to determine the quantity. Remember the Clara Davis study that showed that top quality unprocessed foods always work in favor of your child's growth and development (Chapter 1). Maintaining a positive interaction with your child even if he refuses some foods is your surest strategy to a healthy feeding relationship.

During the second year of life, when your baby's appetite drops normally, you may want to:

— offer very small helpings of individual foods;
— remove uneaten foods without any nasty remarks;
— offer water instead of milk or juice in-between meals to save the appetite for mealtime;
— accept day-to-day changes in eating behavior and appetite.

What are the foods most often refused? Your baby may have been happy with all your food purees during the first 12 months, swallowed the whole range of vegetables with great appetite, then suddenly began to show signs of food refusal. Don't worry, your baby is normal!

Vegetable refusal is the most frequent food refusal in our society. Cooked vegetables are much less popular than raw ones; partially cooked carrot sticks with a yogurt dip can win many adepts.

Red meat refusal comes second and can last for many months while the texture challenge persists. Chicken, tofu, and filleted fish are much easier to chew and swallow.

The list of refusals increases very easily with parental pressure, and the reverse is also true. My own experience with my first daughter is worth a dozen reports. I slowly got into serious negotiation with my very sensitive little girl over every mouthful of vegetables from the time she began walking until the day I gave up insisting—four or five years later! From that moment on, she started to taste and enjoy vegetables, and still does.

What can be done about food allergies?

This is an area of great concern and of growing scientific evidence. Research done in the last 20 years allows us to better understand the issue, but a lot of answers are yet to come. Among accepted facts, we know that:

— Babies are much more vulnerable to adverse food reactions during the first year of life, but skin tests are not useful to determine the offending foods in this age group.

— 58 percent of babies born in families where both parents have a history of allergies have a risk of developing reactions to food.

— 29 percent of babies born in families where only parent has allergies have a risk of developing reactions compared to only 12 percent of babies born in families with no history of allergies.

— Most food reactions occur during the first 12 months.

— Most eliminated foods can be reintroduced by the third year without any risk.

— Symptoms associated with adverse food reactions include diarrhea, vomiting, colic, skin rashes, urticaria, eczema, and chronic nasal congestion, but such symptoms are not always caused by offending foods.

— Foods most often associated with adverse reactions include cow's milk, egg, soy, fruit juice, peanuts, corn, and wheat.

— Any other food introduced in the first three years can potentially cause an adverse reaction in a vulnerable baby.

The good news is that it seems possible to prevent adverse reactions in early months and to delay eventual allergic reactions. The following proposed strategy is especially recommended for infants born into families with a history of food allergies.

From birth on:

a.) Choose to breast-feed for at least six months.

b.) While breast-feeding, eliminate foods in your diet that may cause problems such as milk products and eggs; in doing so, make sure you get sufficient calcium, vitamin D, and protein. (See charts in Chapter 3).

c.) If symptoms occur, eliminate other potential offending foods from your menu such as beef, fish, soy, or peanut butter, but continue breast-feeding as long as you can.

d.) Delay introduction of all solid foods until six months.

When introducing solids:

a.) Introduce one new food every seven days instead of following the regular calendar.

b.) Among infant cereals, leave out wheat cereal until after 12 months.

c.) Avoid mixing foods together before each food component has been introduced separately.

d.) Leave out egg and orange juice until 12 months.

e.) Leave out fish of all kinds and peanut butter until 12 months.

f.) Delay introduction of whole cow's milk until after 12 months, offering breast milk or a protein-hydrolysate-based formula until that age.

After 12 months:

a.) Continue a slow introduction of new foods.

b.) If a reaction occurs, eliminate the suspected food for one to two weeks, and verify if the symptoms disappear.

c.) Reintroduce the eliminated food in a small quantity and observe the reaction; if the symptoms reappear, leave out the offending food for another two or three months, but reintroduce it after that period. In the majority of cases, there is no need or advantage in eliminating a food for a lifetime.

Can a low fat diet prevent high cholesterol in childhood?

The American Academy of Pediatrics recently issued a statement that calls for no low fat diets before the age of two. The conclusion of the NIH Consensus Panel on cholesterol goes in the same direction.

A low-fat intake is not suitable for an infant or a young child; it can even work against the baby's growth and development. Today's recommendation for healthy adults is to lower the total fat intake to 30 percent of total calories. Some programs for cardiac patients, such as Dean Ornish's program for Reversing Heart Disease, suggest an even more drastic drop to 10 percent of total calories. These programs are suitable for adults but present risks for growing children.

Breast milk, which is considered the perfect food for infants for at least six months of life, contains 40 to 50 percent of its calories in the form of fat and 150 mg of cholesterol per liter.

Dietary fat present in breast milk and other foods such as polyunsaturated oils provide essential fatty acids that are critical ingredients for brain development. At birth, the infant's brain weighs about one pound but reaches three pounds by age three. Essential fatty acids are major brain materials acquired during that period.

Cholesterol is also an essential ingredient for nervous system membrane and nerve development in the early years.

For these reasons, the Committee on Nutrition of the Academy of Pediatrics does not recommend a low-fat diet during childhood. It recommends breast milk for at least six months, then whole cow's milk after six months once the baby is eating twelve tablespoons of solid foods per day. The use of skim or partially skim milk is strongly discouraged before 12 months of age. After 12 months, skim milk is tolerated when there is a serious weight problem.

In all other cases, proper growth and development is to be achieved through a healthy menu, not a low-fat diet.

Should babies be screened for cholesterol?

Screening and blood tests should only be considered after two years of age when one parent has had an infarctus before age 50 or has a high-risk cholesterol count. If a two-year-old has a cholesterol measurement over 200 mg/dL after two blood test measurements, dietary changes toward a lower fat intake may be implemented with the help of a registered dietitian.

Will a chubby baby become an obese adult?

Childhood obesity is a growing problem in America, but weight gain during the first year of life is not a predictor of future obesity. At the end of the first year, a baby has normally tripled his or her birth weight and often has a double chin. But most chubby babies return to a normal weight by school age and never become obese.

Excessive weight gain does become a problem around the age of four or five, and studies show that an obese child before school age is quite likely to develop long-term obesity. The family context has a lot to do with such a situation. Heavy parents tend to have obese children more often than lean parents. Genetic and eating habits are both implicated.

A widely spread myth is that obese children always eat more than others. Research has shown that susceptible babies become overweight while eating no more calories than normal-weight babies.

Another myth is that breast-feeding and slow introduction of solid foods prevent long-term obesity. While no one can deny the overall benefits provided by these two excellent feeding practices, no study has ever shown such a long-term result.

The last myth is that dieting can solve the problem! Weight-reduction diets don't work even during childhood. Worse, diet restrictions in early childhood can lead to nutritional deficiencies, lowered body temperature, reduced capacity to fight infections, reduced capacity to be physically active. Such complications are unacceptable and avoidable.

If you are overweight and your two-year-old has a tendency to gain more pounds than is desirable for normal growth, please don't put your child on a diet! The best long-term feeding strategy is to respond very early to your baby's cues by never forcing him/her to finish a bottle or a plate and by helping him/her never to overeat. Five minutes of story telling can very easily replace two chocolate-chip cookies.

If your child is a big eater, slowly increase the fiber content of the menu to provide him/her in the long run with more satisfaction and less calories. Work on a family approach to physical activity to increase everybody's regular energy expenditures. Limit television viewing and walk the dog instead.

Build a family menu around winning foods, and systematically avoid foods that are loaded with added sugar, fat, or salt. If everyone else eats the same healthy meals, it will become much easier for your child to limit heavy snacks and desserts.

If your child has always had a normal weight and suddenly gains 15 pounds in a preschool year, take time to figure out how that has happened. Sudden weight changes often hide emotional discomfort. By tackling the real cause instead of counting calories, your child will learn to avoid misusing food on a long-term basis.

14
Flowers Talk about Nutrition

To help you remember some of the best sources of all the nutrients discussed throughout this book, this chapter leads you through a special garden! Each flower presents a different nutrient, a vitamin, or a mineral. The center of the flower describes the role of each nutrient. The petals indicate major food sources while the leaves translate the child's daily nutritional needs into servings of foods.

You will find energy-producing nutrients such as proteins, carbohydrates, and fats; fat-soluble vitamins A, D, and E; and water-soluble vitamins, including thiamin, riboflavin, niacin, vitamin B6, folic acid, vitamin B12 (called B-complex), and the water-soluble vitamin C.

You will discover good sources of dietary fiber and the key minerals, including iron, calcium, magnesium, and zinc. If your child's menu contains enough of the first three minerals (calcium, iron, and magnesium), the overall quality of his/her menu is guaranteed.

As you will notice, winning foods appear on many flowers and provide more nutrients in every mouthful. Winning foods do not only provide long-term health, but they are fun to cook and fun to eat!

Meats
- beef
- lamb
- veal
- pork
- organ meats

Fish & crustaceans
- sole
- haddock
- perch, cod
- shrimp
- tuna
- salmon

Nuts, cereals, & legumes
- oatmeal, cream of wheat
- shredded wheat
- baked beans
- lentils

Protein
builds tissues, muscles
hair, nails, etc.
•
repairs body tissue
•
supplies energy

Poultry
- chicken
- turkey
- goose
- duck

Eggs and milk products
- whole milk, skim milk
- cheese
- yogurt

Cooking has little effect on protein; save the cooking liquid.

Daily requirements are satisfied with:
20 ounces of milk and 1 ½ ounces of meat or fish or poultry or 2 ounces of tofu

Polyunsaturated fats
- sunflower seeds
- sesame seeds
- pine nuts

Polyunsaturated fats
- sunflower oil
- safflower oil
- sesame oil
- soy oil
- corn oil

Fat
provides energy
•
provides essential
fatty acids
•
promotes absorption
of vitamins A, E, D

Monounsaturated fats
- olive oil
- peanut oil
- canola oil
- avocados
- almonds
- cashews

Saturated fats
- butter
- cheese
- cream & ice cream
- meats
- milk products

Omega-3 fatty acids
- fish
- shell fish
- linseed oil

Daily requirements are satisfied with:
2 teaspoons of polyunsaturated oils and varied sources of fat.

Whole grains
- pot barley
- millet
- oats
- brown rice

Cereal products
- cooked cereals
- dry cereals
- whole-wheat bread
- whole-wheat pasta

Fruits
- bananas
- apples
- oranges
- pears
- kiwis

Carbohydrate

provides energy
•
protects protein

Dried fruits
- raisins
- figs
- prunes
- apricots

Vegetables
- carrots
- green beans
- peppers
- broccoli

*Daily requirements
are satisfied with:*
2 servings of fruit
2 servings of vegetables
3 servings of whole grains
or cereal products

Green vegetables
- spinach
- broccoli
- lettuce
- asparagus

Milk products
- whole milk
- ice cream
- cheddar cheese
- white sauce
- yogurt

Vitamin A
promotes proper growth of bones and teeth
•
maintains a healthy skin
•
promotes good vision

Yellow vegetables
- carrots
- winter squash
- sweet potatoes
- tomatoes

Liver
- lamb
- pork
- beef
- chicken

Colored fruits
- cantaloupe
- peaches
- apricots
- watermelon

Cooking has no effect on this vitamin.

Daily requirements are satisfied with:
1 portion a day of any of these fruits and vegetables plus 1 portion of liver per week.

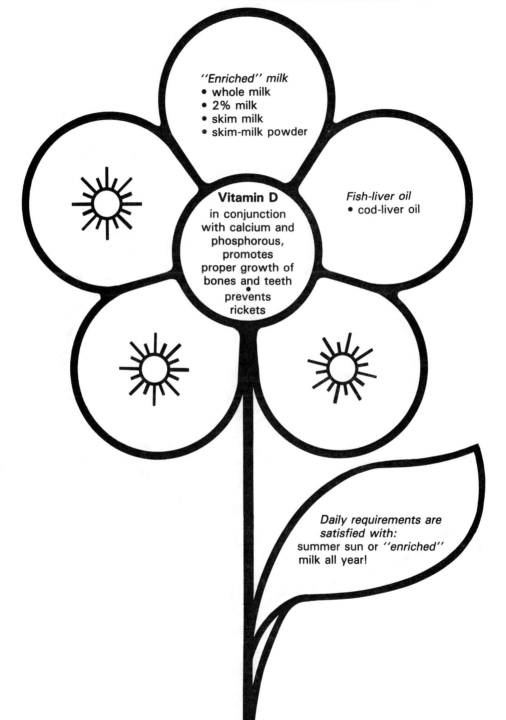

Eggs
- egg yolk

Nuts & legumes
- walnuts
- hazel nuts
- dry peas
- sunflower seeds
- almonds

Vitamin E
prevents food
from going rancid
•
plays role in
intercellular reactions
•
protects cellular
structure

Fruits & vegetables
- spinach
- broccoli
- leeks
- asparagus
- sweet potatoes
- beets
- apples, pears

Vegetable oils
- sunflower
- corn
- soya
- safflower
- cotton seed

Bread & cereals
- whole-wheat bread
- wheat germ
- cornmeal

Daily requirements are satisfied with:
1 serving of fruit plus
1 serving of vegetables

Cooking has no effect
on this vitamin, but
freezing can decrease
the vitamin content.

Fish
- salmon
- oysters
- mackerel

Meats
- pork
- ham
- beef heart

Thiamin
stimulates the appetite
•
regulates the nervous system
•
plays role in intercellular reactions

Milk products
- whole milk
- 2% milk
- white sauce

Cereals
- oatmeal
- whole-wheat bread
- "enriched" cereals
- rice

Nuts & legumes
- baked beans
- almonds
- peanuts

Daily requirements increase with age and child's caloric intake.

Cooking affects thiamin content of food; cook rapidly in small amount of water. Save cooking water.

Cereals
- fortified cereals
- oatmeal

Milk products
- whole milk
- skim milk
- cheddar cheese
- cottage cheese
- ice milk

Green vegetables
- broccoli
- spinach

Riboflavin
maintains healthy
skin and
nervous system

Organ meats
- beef liver
- pork liver
- beef kidney
- beef heart

Milk products
- yogurt
- ice cream
- sherbet
- Ovaltine

Riboflavin is light sensitive. Milk must be kept in opaque containers.

Daily requirements increase with age and child's caloric intake.

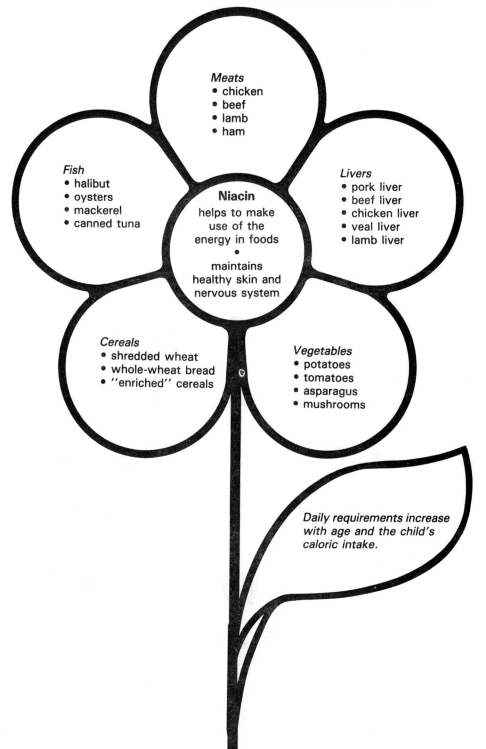

Meats
- chicken
- beef
- lamb
- ham

Fish
- halibut
- oysters
- mackerel
- canned tuna

Niacin

helps to make
use of the
energy in foods
•
maintains
healthy skin and
nervous system

Livers
- pork liver
- beef liver
- chicken liver
- veal liver
- lamb liver

Cereals
- shredded wheat
- whole-wheat bread
- ''enriched'' cereals

Vegetables
- potatoes
- tomatoes
- asparagus
- mushrooms

*Daily requirements increase
with age and the child's
caloric intake.*

Fruits
- bananas
- avocados
- dried figs
- prune juice

Seeds
- sunflower seeds
- sesame seeds

Vitamin B$_6$*
(Pyridoxine)
converts protein to energy
•
participates in development of red blood cells and nerve tissue

Legumes
- white beans
- kidney beans
- lima beans

Whole grains
- brown rice
- wild rice
- wheat bran
- amaranth
- wheatgerm

Fish
- mackerel
- halibut
- haddock
- ocean perch
- tuna

*Processing foods reduces vitamin B$_6$ content

Daily requirements are satisfied with:
1 serving whole-grain cereal and 1 banana

Bread, cereals, nuts, legumes
- whole-wheat bread
- shredded wheat
- cream of wheat
- wheatgerm
- peanuts
- soy beans
- kidney beans
- red beans

Meats & organ meats
- beef
- veal
- pork liver
- chicken livers
- kidneys
- roast beef

Fruits
- nectarines
- oranges
- cantaloupe
- dates
- pineapple
- avocados

Folic Acid

helps in formation of red blood cells
•
plays essential role in intercellular reactions

Vegetables
- spinach
- romaine lettuce
- Brussels sprouts
- beet greens
- asparagus
- broccoli
- sweet potatoes

Eggs & milk products
- whole milk
- yogurt
- cottage cheese
- eggs

Daily requirements are satisfied with:
1 serving of vegetables
1 serving of fruit
1 serving of meat

Cooking and storage for several days without refrigeration has a detrimental effect on this vitamin.

Meats
- roast beef
- veal
- lamb

Organ meats
- beef liver
- beef heart
- chicken liver
- kidneys
- pork liver

Vitamin B_{12}

plays role in intercellular reactions

•

participates in development of red blood cells and nerve tissue

Eggs & milk products
- whole or skim milk
- cottage cheese
- ''hard'' cheese
- eggs

Fish & mollusks
- canned salmon
- mackerel
- oysters

Vitamin B_{12} is not affected by normal cooking procedures.

Daily requirements are satisfied with:
1 portion of meat or 2 cups of milk (16 ozs.).

Vegetables
- green peppers
- tomatoes
- tomato juice
- watercress
- turnips

Small fruits
- strawberries
- raspberries
- blackberries

Vitamin C
maintains healthy gums
•
enhances iron absorption
•
increases resistance to infection
•
prevents scurvy

Cabbage family
- Brussels sprouts
- cauliflower
- uncooked cabbage
- broccoli

Melons
- cantaloupe
- watermelon
- honeydew

Citrus fruits
- oranges
- orange juice
- grapefruit
- grapefruit juice
- lemons
- limes

Daily requirements are satisfied with:
1 serving of any of these fruits or vegetables each day.

Cooking affects vitamin C content: cook rapidly in small amount of water. Save the cooking water.

Soluble fiber
- oat bran
- rice bran
- rolled oats
- legumes
- apples

Fresh fruits & vegetables
- green peas
- kale
- broccoli
- mangoes
- apples
- pears

Dietary Fiber
absorbs water
•
prevents constipation
•
can lower cholesterol
(when soluble)

Dried fruits
- prunes
- raisins
- figs

Insoluble fiber
- wheat bran
- bran cereals
- whole-wheat bread
- wheatgerm

Nuts & seeds
- almonds
- sunflower seeds
- pumpkin seeds
- peanuts
- sesame seeds

Daily requirements are satisfied with:
2 servings of fruit (1 raw)
2 servings of vegetables (1 raw) . . .

3 servings of whole grains or cereal products from either ''Soluble'' or ''Insoluble'' groupings

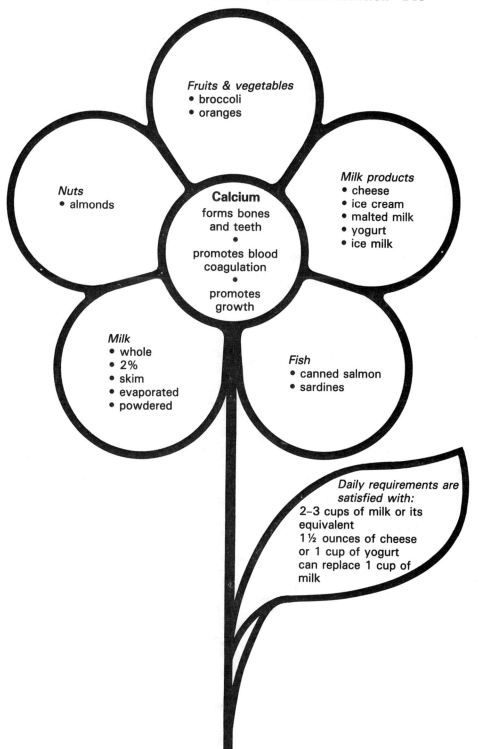

Fruits & vegetables
- broccoli
- oranges

Nuts
- almonds

Milk products
- cheese
- ice cream
- malted milk
- yogurt
- ice milk

Calcium
forms bones
and teeth
•
promotes blood
coagulation
•
promotes
growth

Milk
- whole
- 2%
- skim
- evaporated
- powdered

Fish
- canned salmon
- sardines

Daily requirements are satisfied with:
2–3 cups of milk or its equivalent
1½ ounces of cheese
or 1 cup of yogurt
can replace 1 cup of milk

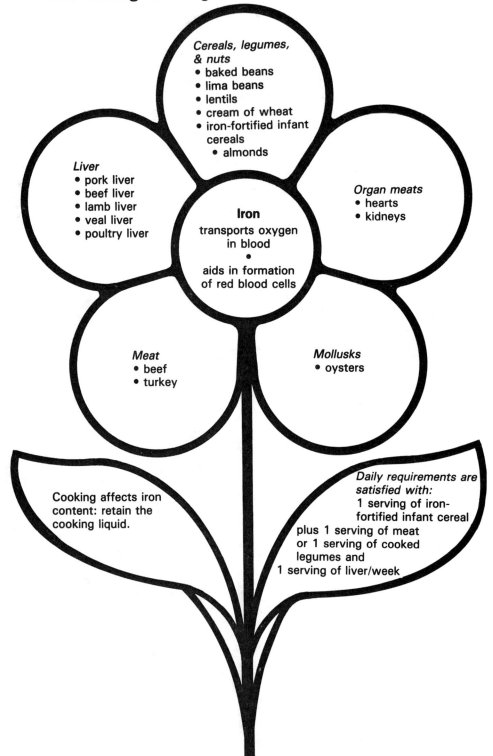

Cereals, legumes, & nuts
• baked beans
• lima beans
• lentils
• cream of wheat
• iron-fortified infant cereals
  • almonds

Liver
• pork liver
• beef liver
• lamb liver
• veal liver
• poultry liver

Iron
transports oxygen in blood
•
aids in formation of red blood cells

Organ meats
• hearts
• kidneys

Meat
• beef
• turkey

Mollusks
• oysters

Cooking affects iron content: retain the cooking liquid.

Daily requirements are satisfied with:
1 serving of iron-fortified infant cereal plus 1 serving of meat or 1 serving of cooked legumes and 1 serving of liver/week

Nuts & seeds
- almonds
- filberts
- macadamias
- peanuts
- pumpkin seeds

Fish
- scallops
- oysters
- mackerel
- halibut
- pollock

Whole grains
- amaranth
- buckwheat
- rolled oats
- brown rice
- wheat bran
- wheatgerm

Magnesium
Promotes resistance to tooth decay
•
Helps relax muscles
•
Works with B vitamins

Legumes
- black beans
- kidney beans
- lima beans
- navy beans
- white beans
- tofu

Vegetables
- spinach
- swiss chard
- acorn squash

Daily requirements are satisfied with:
1 slice of whole-wheat bread and 1 portion of whole grain

80% of magnesium is lost when whole grains are refined. Small amounts are lost into cooking water.

Eggs & milk products
- whole or skim milk
- cheddar cheese
- egg yolk

Bread & cereals
- whole-wheat bread
- rye bread
- oatmeal
- corn
- bran
- wheatgerm

Zinc
important to growth and repair of tissues & intercellular reactions
•
regulates appetite
•
involved in enzyme and hormone formation

Meat and poultry
- beef
- pork
- chicken
- turkey
- liver

Nuts & legumes
- lentils
- dry peas
- peanuts

Mollusks
- oysters

Cooking has little or no effect on the zinc content in foods.

Daily requirements are satisfied with:
1 serving meat
1 serving tofu or legumes
plus 20 ounces milk

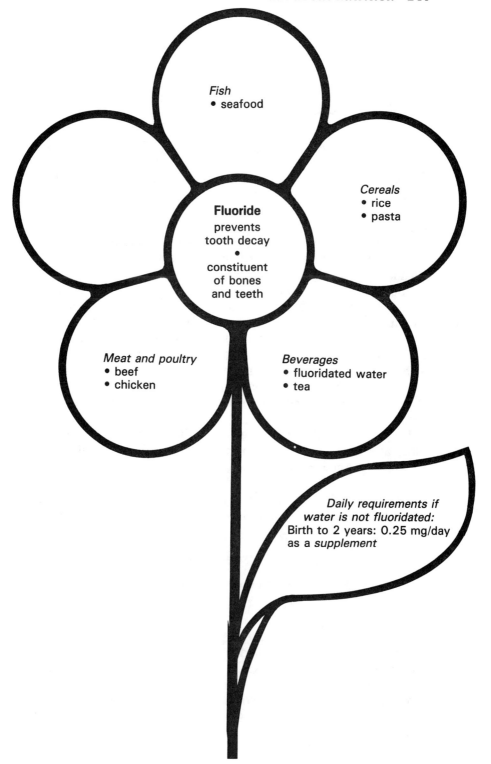

15
The Feeding Challenge
After Nine Months

Feeding a ten- or a fifteen-month-old baby is quite a different challenge from feeding a hungry newborn. New foods are introduced, new texture is introduced, but at the same time a new eating behavior is taking shape.

Your baby's appetite is slowly becoming unpredictable, and mealtime is more tense. You are losing some control over the feeding situation. Your child is gaining power!

Your child is not the only one to play with his food instead of eating it. At 11 months, he has more fun picking up food with his thumb and finger than putting it in his mouth. He can afford to drop food on the floor because he is not as hungry as a few months ago. He expects you to understand the situation and not argue over spoonfuls of food. Your acceptance of his new eating behavior is critical. It can ease a lot of tension and make mealtimes more positive for years to come. Your non-acceptance can ruin your child's relationship to food.

The reality is that a child who eats too little attracts five times as much attention as the one who eats too much. When you think of the growing incidence of obesity during childhood, the reverse should be the case.

An alarming fact is that many parents start misusing food during the preschool years. Food becomes the vehicle for reward or punishment or a means of bargaining:

- vegetables become the passport to dessert;

- sweets become the supreme reward;

- an empty plate wins favors while leftovers are
  seldom accepted.

A child also learns to use food to his advantage, swallowing extra mouthfuls to please, not to respond to hunger. A child is encouraged to overeat while he should be learning to respect his appetite.

Your child's growth rate is slowing down and his appetite follows.

Growth spurts

A child grows in spurts after the first 12 months, and these growth fluctuations affect her whole eating behavior. During the first year of life, your baby gains approximately 10 inches and triples her birth weight. That is a once-in-a-lifetime accomplishment.

A baby born at 7.5 pounds easily weighs 23 pounds at one year and normally weighs 45 pounds at six. This corresponds to a normal growth curve. After 12 months, your child continues to grow but at a much slower pace. Her yearly growth reaches approximately 3 to 4 inches and around 4 to 5 pounds until she attains school age, compared to 10 inches and 16 pounds during the first year of life.

This slower growth rate explains the important drop in appetite but is hard to accept. Your seven-month-old baby who was always ready to swallow food has now developed into what you consider a "fussy eater." What makes things more difficult is that you can never predict a sudden decrease in appetite nor understand the sharp disinterest in food of a fifteen- or twenty-month-old child. That is part of the feeding challenge after nine months.

The only good news is that the younger your child is, the more willing he/she is to try new foods. A study shows that three out of four babies between the ages of twelve and twenty-four months will try new foods while only one in ten toddlers will do the same between the ages of two and four. This interesting fact allows you to introduce small quantities of a wide variety of foods during the transition period between baby food and table food.

Mealtime atmosphere

It can make a difference: a calm and relaxed environment helps your child eat well while a noisy background, including an open television or radio, turns off your child's need for food. A child's attention cannot be split the same way as an adult's. Forgetting to eat is common among young children, especially when lively conversations or harsh noises fill the air.

A regular mealtime schedule promotes better eating. If a meal is served too late, a tired 18-month-old will not eat a bite. Three meals a day are a minimum. Snacks are acceptable as long as they do not replace meals.

Physical comfort at mealtime is also an important appetite enhancer! Make sure your child has:

- a high chair with foot support;
- a table suited to his needs;
- small utensils;

— a good bib;
— a small but wide and unbreakable cup or glass (always half full);
— a bowl or a convex plate rather than a flat one;
— a colorful place mat or tablecloth.

Motor and social development

As months go by, your child's manual abilities and social development evolve.

From 6 to 12 months:

— learns to use his hands;
— displays interest in texture;
— discovers the world with his nose and hands.

At around 15 months:

— he can grasp a spoon and place it on the plate but cannot really fill it up properly;
— once the spoon is close to his mouth, he often holds it upside down;
— often drops his spoon and cup;
— the appetite is decreasing;
— everything but food goes into his mouth.

At 18 months:

— the word "NO" is adopted for all purposes;
— the child drinks well from a cup;
— has some difficulty putting down the cup on the table;
— can now turn the spoon in his mouth;
— growth rate is slow;
— appetite decreases considerably;
— the child loves rituals;
— enjoys finding his place mat, his spoon, etc;
— agrees to be fed when tired.

At 24 months:

— your child can drink from a glass held in one hand;

— can put a spoon in his mouth without turning it;
— has whims;
— is happy with the same food day in and day out;
— needs a more or less rigid schedule;
— still enjoys rituals.

The feeding challenge after nine months requires much more work on your attitude than in the kitchen! Learning to respect your child's messages remains the key to the development of a happy and healthy eater.

16

Transition Menus and Recipes for the Nine-Month-Old and Beyond

The term "transition" is meant to include the whole passage between semi-liquid purees to regular family meals. Some babies breeze through this period quite rapidly. Others are slower, less adventurous. The menus and recipes suggested in this chapter are adapted to the physiological and physical capacities of most nine-month-old babies and beyond, until they reach fifteen to eighteen months. They are easy to prepare but present some particularities:

— The texture is more consistent than the first purees but still softer than regular foods.

— The flavors are still mild but some seasonings are added in moderate amounts such as cinnamon, onions, and parsley. Salt is added to recipes in small quantities after 12 months.

— The variety of foods is much greater. Yogurt, cottage cheese, firm cheese, cooked legumes, tofu, pastas, brown rice, some raw fruit, and vegetables are slowly incorporated into the menu.

Basic foods and portions

Vegetables are steamed over boiling water or cooked in the microwave with very little water. They are fork-mashed after cooking. Some can be grated and served raw, such as carrots and zucchini.

Vegetables are never soaked in water before cooking, as soaking dissolves part of the minerals and vitamins. Cooking water can be kept to later cook rice or pasta.

Plan at least two servings of vegetables a day.

Meats are not easy to sell to babies. They need to be tender and juicy and easy to handle. Some meats are still blended until 12 months. Others are minced. After 12 months, meats are finely cut up, depending on your baby's feeding skills. Fish is poached, flaked, and easy to swallow.

Meat or fish loaves or croquettes are nicely accepted.

Plan one serving a day.

Legumes (beans, lentils, chickpeas) are easily accepted at the end of the first year, when very well cooked. Blend at first, then fork-mash. Tofu can also be blended or gently mashed.

Plan one serving a day for a vegetarian baby. Tofu and legume dishes are good for all babies on a regular basis.

Fruits are popular. Serve as a single puree at first, then blend with other fruit: apple and pear, prunes and apple, pear and peach. Fruits may be lightly poached in fruit juice and fork-mashed, mixed with yogurt or blended with tofu, reduced in a puree, or used to fill up superb jellied desserts. Raw fruit is gradually introduced, such as: small pieces of cantaloupe, honeydew melon, watermelon, slices of kiwi, pear or peach, orange or clementine segments.

Always serve fruit without added sugar to develop your baby's ability to appreciate the real flavor of fresh fruit.

Dilute fruit juice with an equal volume of water to avoid an over-consumption of juice and deficient milk intake.

Plan two or more servings per day, including a vitamin C-rich fruit. (See Vitamin C flower in Chapter 14.)

Whole grains such as brown rice, oatmeal, whole-wheat pasta, and whole-wheat bread provide minerals, protein, and a fair amount of fiber. Infant iron-fortified cereals made with whole grains remain the most nutritious choice in that category during the first 18 months.

Bread can be toasted or cut in strips or fingers. Whole-wheat pita can be served as an alternative. Homemade muffins can be offered. Brown rice and whole-wheat pastas make many happy meals.

Plan at least three servings per day, including a serving of infant iron-fortified cereals every day until 18 months.

Milk and milk products play a major role in your baby's menu. Once your baby is eating approximately three-fourths cup of solid foods per day, she can start drinking whole milk. Babies allergic or intolerant to cow's milk can continue drinking a protein-hydrolysate formula or a soy-based formula (see Chapter 7).

Partially skimmed, 1%, or skim milk are not recommended before the age of 12 months. After that age, you may serve 2% milk without any problem. Totally skimmed milk is only indicated after 12 months when specific problems exist such as a family history of severe cardiovascular disease or a genetically influenced weight problem.

Cottage cheese and yogurt are incorporated in the diet after nine months, once the basic foods have been introduced.

Ice cream or ice milk remain treats to serve on special occasions only!

Chocolate milk is not a good substitute for whole milk. It contains more sugar and more calories.

Plan to serve two and one-half cups (20 ozs.) of milk per day, as a beverage in a cup, in soups, in cereal, or as a snack.

There is honestly no room in your baby's diet for fried foods, processed meats, rich desserts, pastries, and sweets. Even if such foods are part of her environment, try avoiding them without creating tabus. Build a more favorable image around healthier foods.

Some foods are considered risky because they can cause choking:

- popcorn
- nuts and seeds
- chunks in peanut butter
- chewing gum
- hard candies
- raw carrot sticks
- hot dogs
- fruit with seeds, such as grapes

Other foods are good teething foods. They include:
- melba toast or dry bread crusts
- water popsicles

Some foods are easier to grasp and encourage your baby to self-feed. Such good finger foods include:

- cooked vegetable pieces
- cooked pieces of poultry or meat
- cheese cubes
- bread crusts, dry toast
- pieces of poached fruit

All this discussion about adding new foods to your baby's diet improves the variety but does not necessarily increase your baby's appetite. Do not "push" food just because you are excited about a new menu addition. Take into account the nutritional needs of your baby, and do not fill the plate. Some babies ask for more food than others.

Some need more. But if you never force-feed your baby, you will teach him how to respond to his own limits.

The following suggested portions for babies nine to eighteen months can help limit waste and worries.

Infant cereal:	up to ½ cup per day mixed with breast milk, formula, or whole milk.
Fruit:	¼ cup or ¼ of a whole fresh fruit such as a pear or peach.
Jellied fruit dessert:	¼ cup.
Fruit juice:	3 ozs. diluted with an equal amount of water.
Vegetables:	2 tablespoons, cooked or raw grated.
Vegetable soup:	⅓ cup.
Vegetables and meat dinners:	¼ cup.
Fish, meat, or poultry:	1½ ozs.
Whole milk:	½ cup.
Cottage cheese:	¼ cup.
Regular cheese:	½ oz.
Yogurt:	⅓ cup.
Whole-wheat bread:	½ slice.
Brown rice:	¼ cup cooked.
Whole-wheat pasta:	⅓ cup cooked.
Legumes:	¼ cup cooked.
Firm tofu:	1 oz.
Egg:	1 small.

The following menus offer new foods and textures within two balanced eating styles: one with meat and the other with a lacto-ovo vegetarian approach. Main dishes are composed of poultry or meat, legumes, or tofu, cheese and pasta, fish or eggs. The noon meal is the main meal while the night meal is slightly lighter. Whole-grain products are offered most often, such as brown rice, whole-wheat pastas, and whole-wheat bread. Your baby's taste buds are apt to appreciate such flavors. Desserts consist mainly of fresh fruit or fruit purees.

Recipes for foods marked with an asterisk * follow the menus and provide ideas upon which you can expand. The freezer method is often suggested to ease last-minute preparation, but you can always cook smaller quantities just before mealtime if you prefer. The goal is to serve a wide range of nutritious foods at an age when your baby is still willing to try!

The feeding schedule is a simple one. The baby is now ready for the family's timetable and can eat three meals a day plus one milk snack. The feeding capacity of your baby will slowly evolve. On certain days, he will want to feed himself; on other days he demands help! He is slowly learning to drink from a cup and can eat some foods with a spoon.

A 7-Day Menu for the Transition Period
(FROM NINE MONTHS ON)

Day 1

With Meat, Fish or Poultry	Lacto-ovo Vegetarian
BREAKFAST	
orange segments	orange segments
brown rice infant cereal with milk	brown rice infant cereal with milk
whole milk (in cup)	whole milk (in cup)
LUNCH	
poached fresh salmon *	lentils, rice, and vegetables *
fork-mashed zucchini	
whole-wheat bread	whole-wheat bread
pear jellied dessert *	pear jellied dessert *
whole milk (in cup)	whole milk (in cup)
DINNER	
creamed tofu & sesame butter *	creamed tofu & sesame butter *
whole-wheat pita bread	whole-wheat pita bread
banana milk *	banana milk *
SNACK	
whole milk	whole milk

*Recipes available in this book—see Recipe Index.

Day 2

With Meat, Fish, or Poultry	Lacto-ovo Vegetarian
BREAKFAST	

pieces of cantaloupe
oatmeal infant cereal
  with milk
whole milk (in cup)
	pieces of cantaloupe
	oatmeal infant cereal
	  with milk
	whole milk (in cup)

LUNCH	
poached fillet of sole * fork-mashed carrots whole-wheat bread ¼ ripe banana, mashed whole milk (in cup)	pureed legumes and vegetables * whole-wheat bread ¼ ripe banana, mashed whole milk (in cup)
DINNER	

cottage cheese
pureed prunes and
  apples*
whole-wheat bread
whole milk (in cup)
	cottage cheese
	pureed prunes and ap-
	  ples *
	whole-wheat bread
	whole milk (in cup)

SNACK	
whole milk	whole milk

Day 3

With Meat, Fish, or Poultry	Lacto-ovo Vegetarian
BREAKFAST	
apple juice (diluted with water)	apple juice (diluted with water)
barley infant cereal and milk with fresh banana and ground almonds	barley infant cereal and milk with fresh banana and ground almonds
whole milk (in cup)	whole milk (in cup)
LUNCH	
chicken and brown rice	brown rice, vegetables, and cheese *
green beans in small pieces	slices of fresh kiwi
slices of fresh kiwi	whole milk (in cup)
whole milk (in cup)	
DINNER	
cream of green peas * (see cream of vegetable soup)	cream of green peas * (see cream of vegetable soup)
cornbread muffin	cornbread muffin
popsifruits *	popsifruits *
whole milk (in cup)	whole milk (in cup)
SNACK	
whole milk	whole milk

Day 4

With Meat, Fish, or Poultry	Lacto-ovo Vegetarian
BREAKFAST	
apple juice (diluted with water)	apple juice (diluted with water)
oatmeal infant cereal with milk and ground sesame seeds	oatmeal infant cereal with milk and ground sesame seeds
whole milk (in cup)	whole milk (in cup)
LUNCH	
surprise liver and beef loaf *	scrambled tofu *
fork-mashed zucchini	fork-mashed zucchini
whole-wheat bread	whole-wheat bread
cantaloupe in small pieces	cantaloupe in small pieces
whole milk (in cup)	whole milk (in cup)
DINNER	
"two-cheese" macaroni with pieces of broccoli *	"two-cheese" macaroni with pieces of broccoli *
pureed apricots	pureed apricots *
whole milk (in cup)	whole milk (in cup)
SNACK	
whole milk	whole milk

Day 5

With Meat, Fish, or Poultry	Lacto-ovo Vegetarian
BREAKFAST	
orange segments	orange segments
soy infant cereal with milk	soy infant cereal with milk
whole milk (in cup)	whole milk (in cup)
LUNCH	
pureed pork and leeks *	vegetables au gratin *
whole-wheat bread	whole-wheat bread
fruit kebabs *	fruit kebabs *
whole milk (in cup)	whole milk (in cup)
DINNER	
scrambled tofu *	scrambled tofu *
asparagus in small pieces	asparagus in small pieces
½ slice whole-wheat bread	½ slice whole-wheat bread
jellied strawberry dessert *	jellied strawberry dessert *
whole milk (in cup)	whole milk (in cup)
SNACK	
whole milk	whole milk

Day 6

With Meat, Fish, or Poultry	Lacto-ovo Vegetarian
BREAKFAST	

orange segments
soy infant cereal with
  milk
whole milk (in cup)
	orange segments
	soy infant cereal with
	  milk
	whole milk (in cup)

LUNCH	

chicken, brown rice, and
  vegetables *
whole-wheat bread
¼ pear, mashed
whole milk (in cup)
	lentils, brown rice, and
	  vegetables *
	whole-wheat bread
	¼ pear, mashed
	whole milk (in cup)

DINNER	

whole-wheat pasta with
  fresh vegetable sauce
  and grated cheese
¼ ripe banana, mashed
whole milk (in cup)
	whole-wheat pasta with
	  fresh vegetable sauce
	  and grated cheese
	¼ ripe banana, mashed
	whole milk (in cup)

SNACK	
whole milk	whole milk

Day 7

With Meat, Fish, or Poultry	Lacto-ovo Vegetarian
BREAKFAST	
orange juice (diluted with water)	orange juice (diluted with water)
barley infant cereal with milk	barley infant cereal with milk
whole milk (in cup)	whole milk (in cup)
LUNCH	
beef, brown rice, and vegetables *	brown rice, vegetables, and cheese *
whole-wheat bread	whole-wheat bread
apple sauce with cinnamon *	apple sauce with cinnamon *
whole milk (in cup)	whole milk (in cup)
DINNER	
finely grated carrot	finely grated carrot
soft-boiled egg	soft-boiled egg
whole-wheat bread sticks	whole-wheat bread sticks
¼ peach cut in small pieces	¼ peach cut in small pieces
whole milk (in cup)	whole milk (in cup)
SNACK	
whole milk	whole milk

RECIPES

Chicken, Brown Rice, and Vegetables

Easy to prepare with boneless, skinned chicken breast. When your child is able to chew regular food, forget the blender and cut up the chicken in little pieces.

Ingredients

1 boneless, skinned chicken breast
1 teaspoon finely chopped parsley
3 cups water
2 tbsp. minced onion
3 carrots, peeled and finely cut up
1 stalk celery, finely cut up
½ cup uncooked brown rice
1 cup green peas, fresh or frozen

Preparation

Place chicken breast, parsley, water, onion, carrots, and celery in large saucepan. Simmer 15 minutes.

Add brown rice. Simmer 20 minutes.

Add green peas and simmer another 20 minutes until all ingredients are tender and rice is done.

Remove from heat and cool a few minutes only.

Place half the chicken in the blender with ½ cup of the cooking water. Blend, and empty the puree into a large bowl. Repeat with the rest of the chicken.

Drain and fork-mash rice and cooked vegetables. Mix well with the chicken puree.

Pour into glass or microwaveable containers in servings sizes of ¼ cup each. Serve immediately or freeze.

Yield:	about 3 cups, or 12 baby servings of ¼ cup.
Storage life:	2–3 days in refrigerator; 10–12 weeks in the freezer

Beef, Brown Rice, and Vegetables

A dish that can be varied with different grains and different vegetables. It can also be made with minced turkey.

Ingredients

½ cup brown basmati* rice or millet
1 cup leftover vegetable cooking water
and/or plain water
1 lb. lean minced beef
1 teaspoon olive oil
1½–2 cups water
1½ cups finely cut up vegetables:
— ¾ cup each: fresh tomatoes, peeled
and chopped, and finely chopped onions and
green peppers
— ½ cup each: diced carrots, fresh or frozen
green peas, and chopped zucchini
—or any other seasonal vegetable mixture

Preparation

In a small saucepan, put brown rice or millet in cooking water; bring to a boil, then lower heat to simmer approximately 20 minutes.

After 20 minutes, in a medium saucepan, cook meat in olive oil for a few minutes. Add 1½ to 2 cups of water, the selected vegetables, and the half-cooked brown rice or millet. Bring to a boil. Reduce the heat and simmer until vegetables are tender and rice is done.

Remove from heat and cool slightly.

Empty into small glass containers and freeze.

Yield:	3 cups; 1 baby serving before 12 months: ¼ cup
Storage life:	2–3 days in refrigerator; 10–12 weeks in freezer

Reheat in the oven or the microwave; stir the food once during reheating in the microwave. Stir also just before serving.

*Fine-tasting and non-glutinous brown rice.

Pureed Pork and Leeks

Any lean, cooked meat mixed with 1 cup of cooked vegetables can make a similar meal.

Ingredients

1 large leek
5–6 ozs. cooked roast pork, all fat removed
½ cup cooking liquid from the leek

Preparation

Wash and cut the leek, using the white part in this recipe. Save the green part for soups. Steam over boiling water 10–15 minutes or until tender.

Cut pork into small pieces. Put into blender with cooked leek and ½ cup of the cooking liquid. Blend until smooth.

Empty into small containers, ¼ cup for 1 serving. Serve immediately or freeze.

Yield:	2 cups, or 8 baby servings of ¼ cup
Storage life:	2–3 days in the refrigerator; 10–12 weeks in the freezer

Mystery Liver and Beef Loaf

An excellent recipe to sell liver to your child and the rest of the family!

Ingredients

1 lb. chicken livers (from organic animal if possible; calf or lamb liver can also be used)
1 medium onion, quartered
⅔ cup uncooked regular oatmeal
1 cup tomato juice
1¼ lbs. lean minced beef
1 egg
(½ teaspoon salt after 12 months)

Preparation

Preheat oven to 350°F.

Place cleaned, raw liver and onion in the blender. Blend to a smooth puree.

In a large bowl, soak oatmeal in tomato juice for about 10 minutes. Add liver puree, minced beef, egg, and mix well.

Empty into a well-greased loaf pan.

Cook 60–75 minutes.

Let sit 5 minutes before slicing. Cut into small pieces for a baby during the transition period or into slices for an older child.

Yield:	16 baby servings; 8–10 toddler servings
Storage life:	3 days in refrigerator; 10–12 weeks in freezer

Poached Fresh Fish

Babies learn to enjoy the soft and real taste of fish with no batter, no frying fat. Choose fish with low PCB residues as mentioned in the list of ingredients.

Ingredients

¼–½ cup whole milk
1–2 tablespoons finely chopped onion
8 ozs. fillets of fresh fish (choose small farmed fish or ocean fish such as sole, salmon, flounder, grouper, haddock, halibut, monkfish, tuna)

Preparation

Pour ¼ cup milk into a skillet and gently heat. Add onion and simmer several minutes until soft.

Add fish fillets. Cover and cook over low heat 5–10 minutes or until fish is opaque and flaky.

Remove from heat and flake the fish with a fork, making sure all bones are removed.

Store in small containers to serve approximately 1½ ozs. of fish per serving; add a small amount of milk and onions. Cover and freeze or serve immediately.

Reheat in 400°F. oven for about 10 minutes or in the microwave for 1 minute at high. Stir once during reheating in the microwave and stir just before serving.

Yield: 5 baby servings of 1½ ozs.

Storage life: 2–3 days in refrigerator; 4–6 weeks in freezer

Basic White Sauce (medium thickness)

Can be prepared on the stove or in the microwave.

Ingredients

2 tablespoons oil
2 tablespoons whole-wheat, all-purpose flour
½ cup whole milk
½ cup chicken stock or leftover vegetable cooking liquid

Preparation

On the stove: In a saucepan, mix oil and flour and heat for a few minutes. Gradually add milk and stock, stirring constantly until the sauce thickens. Cook 1 additional minute.

In the microwave: in a 4-cup glass bowl, heat the oil on high power for 30 seconds. Add flour and mix until smooth. Add liquid gradually, stirring constantly until smooth. Cook in microwave on high for 3–6 minutes or until sauce is thickened and smooth, stirring every 2 minutes.

Cool and use immediately or store in refrigerator or freezer.

Yield:	1 cup
Storage life:	3–4 days in refrigerator; 4 weeks in freezer

Brown Rice, Vegetables, and Cheese

Cheese can be replaced with tofu or mixed with it, half and half. Adjust seasonings with fresh herbs.

Ingredients

½ cup white sauce, medium thickness (no salt added to sauce before 12 months). Recipe, pg. 171
½ cup cooked brown rice
½ cup fork-mashed vegetables (asparagus, zucchini, squash, carrots)
6 tablespoons grated, partially skimmed mozzarella cheese

Preparation

Reheat white sauce in glass bowl in microwave. Mix in all ingredients except cheese; stir well.

Freeze in individual portions of ¼ cup each or refrigerate to serve within a few days.

Reheat in a double boiler or in the microwave. Stir once during reheating in the microwave. Stir also just before serving, and add 1 teaspoon of grated cheese onto each portion.

Yield: 1½ cups, or 6 baby servings of ¼ cup

Storage life: 2–3 days in refrigerator; 3–4 weeks in freezer

Scrambled Tofu

Looks like scrambled eggs and tastes even better!

Ingredients

4 ozs. firm tofu (silken Japanese type)
2 tablespoon minced onion
1 teaspoon light tamari sauce
¼ teaspoon turmeric (a spice that colors the mixture yellow when cooked)
2 teaspoons oil

Preparation

In a bowl, mash tofu; add next 3 ingredients and mix well.
In skillet, pour oil and heat over medium heat.
Add ingredients from bowl and cook 5 minutes or until warm throughout and lightly color yellow. Serve immediately.

Yield: 2-3 baby servings

Storage life: 2 to 3 days in refrigerator

Pureed Legumes with Vegetables

A good vegetarian dish that introduces legumes into the child's menu. Divide recipe by two or three to begin with.

Ingredients

1 cup warm white sauce, medium thickness
(see recipe pg. 171)
1 cup well-cooked legumes† (dried peas, red kidney beans, chickpeas, soy beans) pureed in blender, food processor, or food mill
½ cup fork-mashed vegetables (carrots, zucchini, or asparagus)

Preparation

Reheat white sauce in large bowl in the microwave. Add pureed legumes and vegetables. Mix well.

Divide into serving portions of ¼ cup. Pour into glass or microwaveable containers.

Store in freezer or in refrigerator for a few days.

Reheat in double boiler or in microwave, a minute or so. Stir once during reheating in microwave and stir also just before serving.

Yield: 2½ cups, or 10 baby servings of ¼ cup

Storage life: 2–3 days in refrigerator; 4–6 weeks in freezer

†Canned, drained, and rinsed kidney beans or chickpeas can be used.

Lentils, Brown Rice, and Vegetables

Another nutritious vegetarian meal with lentils.

Ingredients

½ cup well-cooked brown or green lentils
¼ cup cooked brown rice
½ cup white sauce, medium thickness (see
recipe above)
¼ cup cooked and finely cut vegetables:
carrots, green beans.

Preparation

Reheat white sauce in a large bowl in the microwave.

Add cooked lentils, brown rice, and vegetables. Mix well.

Pour into small glass or microwaveable containers in serving portions of ¼ cup.

Serve immediately or freeze.

Yield:	1 ½ cups, or 6 baby servings of ¼ cup
Storage life:	2–3 days in refrigerator; 3–4 weeks in freezer

Cream of Vegetable Soup

Prepare in minutes with the best vegetables on the market. Can be made with soy milk instead of whole milk. A nice way to sell invisible but good-tasting vegetables.

Ingredients

½ cup whole milk (2% milk after 12 months if desired)
¼ – ½ cup raw or frozen vegetables: cauliflower, broccoli flowers, asparagus, green peas, green string beans
½ slice whole-wheat bread
1 teaspoon olive or sunflower oil

Preparation

Steam vegetables over boiling water or cook a few minutes in the microwave.

In the blender, pour vegetables, cooking water, milk, bread, and oil. Blend for 30 seconds. Add more liquid is needed.

Reheat and serve. Freeze leftovers if desired.

Yield:	1 ½ cups, or 4 baby servings
Storage life:	3–4 days in refrigerator; 1 month in freezer

Two-Cheese Macaroni

Babies love pastas like the rest of the family!

Ingredients

2 cups cooked whole-wheat macaroni blended
with ¾ cup whole milk
2 eggs
1 cup whole milk (2% or 1% after 12 months)
1 cup light cottage cheese
4–6 tablespoons grated, partly skimmed
mozzarella cheese
2 teaspoons butter or olive oil
(½ teaspoon salt after 12 months)

Preparation

In blender, beat eggs; add milk, cottage cheese, grated cheese, and butter or oil. Blend well.

Pour mixture onto the cooked, blended macaroni. Mix well.

Place in small glass or microwaveable containers in ¼-cup servings.

Reheat in the oven or in the microwave. If frozen, remove from freezer and cook in a 350°F. oven for about 40 minutes or defrost and reheat in the microwave, stirring just before serving.

Yield: 3 cups, or 12 baby
servings of ¼ cup

Storage life: 2–3 days in
refrigerator;
4–6 weeks in freezer

Creamed Tofu and Sesame Butter

Delightfully smooth and tasty! Can be done with peanut butter as well.

Ingredients

4 ozs. firm tofu (silken Japanese type)
½ cup dark sesame butter†
2 teaspoons honey

Preparation

In blender or food processor, put tofu and sesame butter. Blend until smooth. Add 1 teaspoon honey and taste before adding more.

Serve as a spread with whole-wheat pita bread or as a dip with pieces of fresh fruit.

Yield: 1 cup

Serving size: 1–2 tablespoons

Storage life: 1 week in refrigerator

†Dark sesame butter is prepared with *whole* sesame seeds while "tahini" is prepared with *hulled* sesame seeds. The former contains much more calcium than the latter.

Vegetables au Gratin

Easy to prepare and to vary, according to the freshest vegetables on the market.

Ingredients

1 cup white sauce, medium thickness (see recipe above)
⅓ cup grated mozzarella cheese
1 cup cooked carrots, fork-mashed
1 cup cooked green vegetables, fork-mashed or pureed (broccoli, green peas, asparagus)

Preparation

Reheat white sauce in a large bowl in microwave or double boiler.

Add grated cheese and let it melt by stirring a few minutes. Add vegetables and mix well.

Serve immediately. Pour leftovers in small glass or microwaveable containers. Refrigerate or freeze.

Reheat in double boiler or in a few minutes in microwave. Stir just before serving.

Yield: 3 cups, or 12 baby servings of ¼ cup

Storage life: 2–3 days in refrigerator; 4–6 weeks in freezer

Jellied Fruit Dessert

Much more flavorful than commercial jellied desserts, filled with vitamin-rich fruit juice and purees. Try:
orange juice and banana puree; or
white grape juice and pear puree; or
apple juice and strained strawberry puree

Ingredients

¼ cup cold water
1 package unflavored gelatin (Knox type)
½ cup boiling water
1 cup fruit juice
1 cup fruit puree (fresh fruit pureed in blender with or without juice)

Preparation

Pour cold water in medium bowl. Sprinkle gelatin over water and allow to swell. Add boiling water and dissolve gelatin. Add fruit juice and fruit puree; mix well.
If desired, pour into small, individual bowls.
Refrigerate a few hours, until gelatin is firm.

Yield:	2¾ cups
Baby serving:	2–3 tablespoons
Storage life:	2–3 days in refrigerator

Fruit Kebabs

Pretty to look at and easy to prepare. Vary the fruit: use pitted prunes instead of peaches, pears instead of oranges, and enjoy! When your baby is older, add a third fruit such as banana or kiwi slices.

Ingredients

1 fresh peach or nectarine, peeled and quartered
1 orange in segments

Preparation

Thread fruit onto 2 bamboo or wooden skewers, alternating between pieces of peach and segments of oranges.
Keep in refrigerator until ready to serve.

Yield: 2 kebabs (one for you and one for baby)

Banana Milk

A dessert in a glass or cup.

Ingredients

1 small banana, cut in pieces
½ cup whole milk
drop of vanilla

Preparation

Place banana and milk in blender and blend well. Add vanilla. Pour into cup or glass.

If not serving immediately, refrigerate and serve cold.

Yield: 1 cup

Popsifruits

Delicious sorbet-like homemade popsicles. Can be served in a dish or as a popsicle. Try orange, grape juice, or apple juice. All flavors are delightful.

Ingredients

2 cups plain yogurt
1 can, 6¼-oz., of frozen, unsweetened fruit juice.

Preparation

In a blender, pour yogurt and undiluted fruit juice. Blend until smooth.

Pour mixture into popsicle molds or individual glass dishes. Freeze.

To serve, run popsicle under very hot water to loosen it, or remove bowl from freezer 15–30 minutes before serving so that popsicle acquires a good consistency.

Yield: 10 popsicles

17
Learning to Love Good Foods

The first few years of a child's life are the years in which he or she explores the world. They are years filled with new visual, auditory, gustatory, and olfactory experiences.

A child slowly discovers colors, textures, shapes, smells, and tastes. After the first few months, his eyes are attracted to the "red" toy rather than the little beige dog, to the orange carrot, rather than green beans. His fingers react to different textures and can differentiate between a plush doggy, a smooth ball, and a rag doll. His taste buds experience a whole range of new tastes, and even at this age, he makes his likes and dislikes known (mashed bananas are eaten faster than pureed meats). His ears recognize the music-box's melody. His nose learns to sniff and enjoy pleasant smells.

Everything that is taken in and retained during the first years of life is accomplished through the baby's senses. The more opportunities a child has to see, touch, taste, smell, and hear, the more he gets to know the world around him and the better prepared he is to deal with it.

Senses must be exercised just as muscles must be exercised. The child grows to love the things he knows: the pretty toy he looks at, the cat he strokes, the melon he tastes, the rose he smells, the song he hears!

Food is a part of the child's world. The more opportunities he has to learn about different foods, the greater the chances that he will like them.

Always keeping the objective of forming good eating habits in mind, this last chapter suggests activities, games, and experiences for the child that will enable him to discover and appreciate a wide variety of foods while having fun.

Let's visit the market or the farm
(two to two-and-a-half or older)

It is a real pleasure for a child to go to the supermarket with his mother. Sitting in a "silver" carriage, she discovers a whole new world of foods. This experience can be both pleasant for the mother and valuable for the child, even if it only takes place occasionally.

It is better to go shopping for food after having eaten. This spares the mother the wails of a hungry child. In the same vein, buying sweets or cookies to calm the over-excited child must not be done. If it's time for her snack, a child should be given an apple or a small package of raisins to nibble on.

During this visit, the child learns by watching her mother fill her shopping cart. In her mind, the food that mother buys is good food: good for the family and good for her! If all she sees is canned goods, frozen foods, and prepared dishes, she will not learn very much and will get a very poor idea of what constitutes a good diet.

If, on the other hand, the mother buys basic foods (meat, fruit and vegetables, cereals, and milk products), and she explains why she is buying such-and-such a vegetable or cut of meat (to make a salad, to prepare some casserole), the child will feel that she is actively participating and will be very happy. Every now and then, the infant should be allowed to make the choice between two kinds of cheeses, two vegetables, or two fruits or fruit juice of equal nutritional value. If she has had a say in the actual choice of the food, she will be interested in getting to know it and will not refuse it when it appears on her plate.

Open-air, or "farmer's," markets
(suitable for three-year-olds)

A family visit to this type of market at the height of the season is a treat that should be fully taken advantage of. Between June and mid-October, it is possible to purchase fruits and vegetables in open-air markets. This is one activity a child should not miss.

He can savor the smell of fresh fruits and vegetables and will learn to recognize the characteristics of good vegetables or fruit: the whiteness of the cauliflower, the firmness of green peppers, the shiny skin of eggplants and zucchini, the deep colors of strawberries, and so on.

What a pleasure to taste the first carrots of the season!

There is no substitute for the smell of vegetables and fruits in season, and this is the perfect way to give our children a taste for them.

The fish market
(suitable for three-year-olds or older)

The fish market presents nature's wonders to the curious and attentive child. No need to visit the ocean to see molluscs or crustaceans, mussels, clams, oysters, scallops, or snails. How surprising to see "green" lobsters swimming in salt water tanks and yet find them "red" in the refrigerated display section. Or how about discovering frog's legs . . . or better still, an octopus!

Fish is no exception to the rule. A child will like it if he has acquired a taste while very young and if his mother prepared it so that all of its flavor is retained.

To double this pleasure, let the child choose his own favorite fish once in a while!

The farm
(suitable for three-year-olds and over)

To gather a still-warm freshly laid egg in the hen house, to see a cow being milked, to discover a pig's curly tail, to run in wheat fields, to go to a corn roast, to climb an apple tree and pick a ripe apple — these are but a few of the experiences that teach a child about the origins of his food. Throughout the summer, many farms open their doors to welcome families interested in sharing these experiences firsthand.

A walk in the country
(for three-year-olds or older)

With a pair of good sharp eyes and a little luck, one can usually discover several edible plants growing wild during a simple walk in the country. Every month of the summer has something different to offer. In May you will find the young shoots known as "fiddleheads," a delicious and tender vegetable that is cooked in the same way as green string beans. In June dandelion greens make an excellent salad and are rich in vitamin C. July brings wild strawberries and wild raspberries. In August tiny, delicious, flavorful blueberries are available. Autumn brings various nuts, walnuts, and hazel nuts, which are simply delicious — not to mention chestnuts.

A child soon learns to appreciate the flavor of these edible wild plants, which she has picked for herself in the countryside.

Let's try planting our own vegetables

All that is needed to grow one's own vegetables is earth, water, sunshine, and a lot of tender love and care. Even in the heart of the big city, a child can still enjoy the fun of a vegetable garden.

Cherry tomatoes
(for three-year-olds and older)

At the end of March, cherry tomato plants are available at garden stores. They can be planted in a ten-inch-diameter pot; the pot is then placed in a sunny window. The aspiring young gardener is then responsible for its care and watering — carefully and tactfully guided and supervised, of course. When the warm weather arrives, the pot is put outdoors on a terrace or balcony in a sunny spot. The plants can then be trained to climb on a trellis or stake. If the young gardener has done his job well, he can proudly harvest and eat several miniature tomatoes.

Little peas grow into big peas
(for three-year-olds or older)

By sowing green peas, the child is able to observe every step in the development of a vegetable: seed, leaves, flowers, pods, and the green peas themselves. This experience is truly worthwhile!

As soon as spring has arrived, a child can sow two or three pea seeds in a ten-inch-diameter pot, filled with planting soil. Place the pot near a sunny window and water regularly when the soil becomes dry.

At the end of a few weeks, the child will notice the seedling and then some leaves. As soon as it is warm enough outside, place the pot in a warm, sunny corner of the garden or outside on the balcony, near a fence or a trellis, since this is a climbing plant.

The child will then be able to watch the successive stages of its growth — the flowers and then the pods, inside of which the peas themselves will slowly form.

Words can hardly express a child's happiness as he tastes the peas (raw or cooked) that he himself planted.

Let's make homemade bread
(activity for four-year-olds and older)

What a thrill to discover in your own kitchen that yeast makes dough rise! And what a splendid smell hot bread has as it comes from the oven. What can be more lovely than devouring it warm!

A child who has walked in a wheat field, has watched the grain being ground, and has helped to make the bread has had a unique and unforgettable experience!

Bread-making is simple. However, four hours have to be set aside for the dough to rise and for baking. Early morning or early afternoon is the ideal time to start work on the recipe that follows. The baking will coincide with mealtime so that tasting the bread will not spoil a child's appetite.

Whole-Wheat Bread

Ingredients

5–6 cups whole-wheat flour
1 cup boiling water
2 teaspoons salt
1 tablespoon butter
5 tablespoons powdered skim milk
¼ cup honey
¾ cup cold water
1 envelope of yeast, sprinkled over ¼ cup lukewarm water

Preparation (the mother should carry out the first six steps)

1. Place honey, margarine, and salt in a large bowl.
2. Pour in boiling water and mix well.
3. Add cold water and mix until preparation is lukewarm
4. Add the soaked yeast and 3 cups flour (1 cup at a time). Mix until mixture is smooth.
5. Add powdered milk and beat for 2 minutes.
6. Add remaining flour and mix well.
7. Knead dough. Show the child how to do this, and let her try it for a few minutes.
8. When the dough has been well kneaded, brush a little vegetable oil over top of dough, cover with a damp cloth, and let dough rise until it has doubled in volume.
9. Once dough has doubled, show child the change; let her punch the dough in center and watch it sink down.
10. Knead dough again with help of child and shape into 2 small loaves. Place in well-greased bread pans, cover, and let rise until double in volume. Alternatively: divide dough into small pieces and let child "sculpt" her own little loaves. Cover with damp cloth and let rise until double in volume in a drafty area, while explaining to child what yeast is and how it makes dough rise.
11. When dough has doubled in bulk, cook in a 350°F. oven until loaves are golden and crusty (45–60 minutes).

Bibliography

American Academy of Pediatrics, Committee on Drugs. "Transfer of Drugs and Other Chemicals Into Human Milk." *Pediatrics* 84 (November 1989): 924–936.

American Academy of Pediatrics, Committee of Environmental Hazards. "PCBs in Breast Milk." *Pediatrics* 62 (September 1978).

American Academy of Pediatrics, Committee on Nutrition. "Hypoallergenic Infant Formulas." *Pediatrics* 83 (June 1989): 1068–1069.

American Academy of Pediatrics, Committee on Nutrition. "Indications for Cholesterol Testing in Children." *Pediatrics* 83 (January 1989): 141–142.

American Academy of Pediatrics, Committee on Nutrition. "Iron-Fortified Infant Formulas." *Pediatrics* 84 (December 1989): 1114–1115.

American Academy of Pediatrics, Committee on Nutrition. "Fluoride Supplementation." *Pediatrics* 77 (May 1986): 758–761.

American Academy of Pediatrics, Committee on Nutrition. "Follow-up or Weaning Formulas." *Pediatrics* 83 (June 1989): 1067.

American Academy of Pediatrics, Committee on Nutrition. "On the Feeding of Supplemental Foods to Infants." *Pediatrics* 65 (June 1980): 1178–1181.

American Academy of Pediatrics, Committee on Nutrition. "Plant Fiber Intake in the Pediatric Diet." *Pediatrics* 67 (April 1981): 572–575.

American Academy of Pediatrics, Committee on Nutrition. "Prudent Lifestyle for Children: Dietary Fat and Cholesterol." *Pediatrics* 78 (September 1986): 521–525.

American Academy of Pediatrics, Committee on Nutrition. "Soy-Protein Formulas: Recommendations for Use in Infant Feeding." *Pediatrics* 72 (September 1983): 359–363.

American Academy of Pediatrics, Committee on Nutrition. "The Use of Whole Cow's Milk in Infancy." *Pediatrics* 72 (August 1983): 253–255.

American Academy of Pediatrics, Committee on Nutrition. "Use of Oral Fluid Therapy and Posttreatment Feeding Following Enteritis in Children in a Developed Country." *Pediatrics* 75 (February 1985): 358–361.

American Academy of Pediatrics, Committee on Nutrition. "Vitamin and Mineral Supplement Needs in Normal Children in the United States." *Pediatrics* 66 (December 1980): 1015–1021.

Anderson, G.H., et al. "Medical Progress. Age of Introduction of Cow's Milk to Infants." *Journal of Pediatric Gastroenterology and Nutrition* 4 (1985): 692–698.

Avery, M.E., and Snyder, J.D. "Oral Therapy for Acute Diarrhea." *The New England Journal of Medicine* 323 (September 1990): 891–893.

Babich, H., and Davis, D.L. "Food Tolerances and Action Levels: Do They Adequately Protect Children?" *BioScience* 31 (June 1981): 429–438.

Ballard, P. "Breast-Feeding for the Working Mother." *Issues in Comprehensive Pediatric Nursing* 6 (1983): 249–259.

Barness, L.A. "Adverse Effects of Overdosage of Vitamins and Minerals." *Pediatrics in Review* 8 (July 1986): 20–24.

Beaton, G.H. "Nutritional Needs of the Pregnant and Lactating Mother." In The Mother-Child Dyad – Nutritional Aspects, Symposium of the Swedish Nutrition Foundation XIV. Stockholm: Almquist and Wiksell, 1979.

Benkov, K.J., and LeLeiko, N.S. "A Rational Approach to Infant Formulas." *Pediatrics Annals* 16 (March 1987): 225–230.

Bock, S.A. "Prospective Appraisal of Complaints of Adverse Reactions to Foods in Children During the First 3 Years of Life." *Pediatrics* 79 (May 1987): 683–688.

Bowles, B.C., and Williamson, B.P. "Pregnancy and Lactation Following Anorexia and Bulimia." *Journal of Obstetric Gynecologic and Neonatal Nursing* 19:3 (June 1990): 243–248.

Brewer, M.M.; Bates, M.R.; and Vannoy, L.P. "Postpartum Changes in Maternal Weight and Body Fat Depots in Lactating vs. Nonlactating Women." *American Journal of Clinical Nutrition* 49 (1989): 259–265.

Brown, L.W. "Commentary: Infant Botulism and the Honey Connection." *The Journal of Pediatrics* 94 (February 1979).

Bruch, Hilde. *Eating Disorders.* New York: Basic Book Publishers, 1973.

Calabrese, Edward G. "Polychlorinated Biphenyls" and "B-Vitamins." In *Nutrition and Environmental Health,* Vol. 1, "The Vitamins." New York: John Wiley and Sons, 1980.

Chandra, R.K.; Singh, G.; and Shridhara, B. "Effect of Feeding Whey Hydrolysate, Soy and Conventional Cow Milk Formulas on Incidence of Atopic Disease in High Risk Infants." *Annals of Allergy* 63 (August 1989): 102–106.

Cravioto, J.; Birch, H.G.; Delicardie, E.R.; and Rosales, I. "The Ecology of Infant Weight Gain in a Pre-Industrial Society." *Acta Paediatrica Scandinavia* 56 (1967): 71–84.

Crawford, M.A., et al. "Milk Lipids and Their Variability." *Current Medical Research and Opinion* 4 (1976).

Cunningham, A.S. "Morbidity in Breast-Fed and Artificially Fed Infants, II." *Journal of the American Dietetic Association* 75 (August 1979).

Deeming, S.B., and Weber, C.J. "Trace Minerals in Commercially Prepared Baby Foods." *Journal of the American Dietetic Association* 75 (August 1979).

Dreikeurs, Rudolf. *Children: The Challenge.* New York: Duell, Sloan and Perce, 1964.

Duncan, B., et al. "Iron and the Exclusively Breast-Fed Infant from Birth to Six Months." *Journal of Pediatric Gastroenterology and Nutrition* 4 (1985): 421–425.

Food and Nutrition Board. *Recommended Dietary Allowances.* Washington, D.C.: National Academy Press, 1989.

Finberg, L. "Summary. The Weaning Process." *Pediatrics* (supplement 1985): 214–215.

Fitzgerald, J.F. "Constipation in Children." *Pediatrics in Review* 8 (April 1987): 299–302.

Fomon, S.J. *Infant Nutrition,* 2nd edition. Toronto: W.B. Saunders, 1974.

Fomon, S.J., et al. "Skim Milk in Infant Feeding." *Acta Paediatrica Scandinavia* 66 (1977).

Foucard, T. "Development of Food Allergies with Special Reference to Cow's Milk Allergy." *Pediatrics* 75 (supplement 1985): 177–181.

Gaull, G.E., et al. "Significance of Growth Modulators in Human Milk." *Pediatrics* 75 (January 1985): 142–145.

Glueck, S.J., et al. "Plasma and Dietary Cholesterol in Infancy." *Metabolism* 21 (1972): 1121.

Gortmaker, S.L., et al. "Increasing Pediatric Obesity in the United States." *American Journal of Disease of Children* 141 (May 1987): 535–540.

Government of Canada: *Environment Canada and Health.* Priority Substances List Assessment Report no. 1, Polychlorinated Dibenzodioxins and Polychlorinated Dibenzofurans. Canada: Minister of Supply and Services Canada, 1990.

Greer, F.R., et al. "Water Soluble Vitamin D in Human Milk: a Myth." *Pediatrics* 69 (February 1982).

Grunwaldt, E.; Bates, T.; and Guthrie, D.J. "The Onset of Sleeping through the Night in Infancy." *Pediatrics* 26 (October 1960): 667–668.

Hall, B. "Changing Composition of Human Milk and Early Development of an Appetite Control." *Lancet* (April 1975): 779–81.

Hambidge, K.M., et al. "Plasma Zinc Concentrations of Breast-Fed Infants." *Journal of Pediatrics* 94 (April 1979).

Hambraeus, L. "Proprietary Milks versus Human Breast Milk. A Critical Approach from the Nutritional Point of View." *Pediatric Clinic of North America* 24 (1977).

Hamburger, R.N. *Food Intolerance in Infancy, Allergology, Immunology, and Gastroenterology.* New York: Raven Press, 1989.

Higginbottom, M.C., et al. "A Syndrome of Methylmalonic Aciduria, Homocystinuria, Megaloblastic Anemia and Neurological Abnormalities in Vitamin B12 Deficient Breast-Fed Infant of a Strict Vegetarian." *The New England Journal of Medicine* 299 (1978).

Hyams, J.S., and Leichtner, A.M. "Apple Juice. An Unappreciated Cause of Chronic Diarrhea." *American Journal of Disease of Children* 139 (May 1985): 503–505.

Institute of Medicine. *Nutrition During Pregnancy.* Washington, D.C.: National Academy Press, 1990.

Jakobsson, I., and Lindberg, T. "Cow's Milk Proteins Cause Infantile Colic in Breast-Fed Infants: A Double-Blind Crossover Study." *Pediatrics* 71 (February 1983): 268–271.

Jelliffe, B.D., and Jelliffe, E.F.P. *Human Milk in the Modern World.* Toronto: Oxford University Press, 1978.

Katcher, A.L., and Lanese, M.G. "Breast-Feeding by Employed Mothers: A Reasonable Accommodation in the Work Place." *Pediatrics* 75 (April 1985): 644–647.

Kerr, G.M., et al. "Sodium Concentration of Homemade Baby Foods." *Pediatrics* 62 (September 1978).

Klaper, M. *Pregnancy, Children, and the Vegan Diet.* Florida: Gentle World, Inc., 1987.

Klaus, M.H., and Kennel, J.H. *Maternal-Infant Bonding.* St. Louis: C.V. Mosby, 1976.

"Lactation and Composition of Milk in Undernourished Women." *Nutrition Reviews* 33 (February 1975).

Lascari, A.D. "Early Breast-Feeding Jaundice: Clinical Significance." *Journal of Pediatrics* 108 (January 1986): 156–158.

Lawrence, R.A. *Breastfeeding: A guide for the Profession,* third edition. C.V. Mosby, 1989.

Lawrence, R.A. "Breastfeeding." *Pediatrics in Review* 11 (December 1989): 163–171.

Lee, E.J., and Heiner, D.C. "Allergy to Cow Milk-1985." *Pediatrics in Review* 7 (January 1986): 195–203.

Leung, A.K.C., and Robson W.L.M. "Acute Diarrhea in Children. What to do and not to do." *Postgraduate Medicine* 86 (December 1989): 161–174.

Lothe, L.; Linberg, T.; and Jakobsson, I. "Cow's Milk Formula as a Cause of Infantile Colic: A Double Blind Study." *Pediatrics* 70 (July 1981): 7–10.

Lozoff, B., and Zuckerman, B. "Sleep Problems in Children." *Pediatrics in Review* 10 (July 1988): 17–24.

Macknin, M.L.; Medendorp, V.B.; and Maier, M.C. "Infant Sleep and Bedtime Cereal." *American Journal of Disease of Children* 143 (September 1989): 1066–1068.

Martinez, G.A., and Nalczienski, J.P. "1980 Update: The Recent Trend in Breast-Feeding." *Pediatrics* 67 (February 1981).

Mellies, M.J., et al. "Effects of Varying Maternal Dietary Cholesterol and Phytosterol in Lactating Women and Their Infants." *American Journal of Clinical Nutrition* 31 (August 1978).

Mes, J., et al. "Polychlorinated Biphenyls and Organochlorine Pesticides in Milk and Blood of Canadian Women During Lactation." *Archives of Environmental Contamination and Toxicology* 13 (1984): 217–223.

Morse, W., et al. "Mothers' Compliance with Physicians' Recommendations on Infant Feeding." *Journal of the American Dietetic Association.* 75 (August 1979).

Morton, R.E.; Nysenbaum, A.; and Price, K. "Iron Status in the First Year of Life." *Journal of Pediatric Gastroenterology and Nutrition* 7 (1988): 707–712.

Motohara K.; Endo F.; and Matsuda I. "Vitamin K Deficiency in Breast-Fed Infants at One Month of Age." *Journal of Pediatric Gastroenterology and Nutrition.* 5 (1986): 931–933.

Nelson, S.E., et al. "Lack of Adverse Reactions to Iron-Fortified Formula." *Pediatrics* 81 (March 1988): 360–364.

Orga, S.S., and Orga, P.L. "Immunological Aspects of Human Colostrum and Milk, I and II." *Journal of Pediatrics* 92 (April 1978).

Perkin, J.E. *Food Allergies and Adverse Reactions.* Gaithensburg, Md.: Aspen Publishers, Inc., 1990.

Picciano, M.F., and Guthrie, J. "Copper, Iron, Zinc Contents of Mature Human Milk." *American Journal of Clinical Nutrition* 29 (1976).

Picciano, M.F., et al. "The Cholesterol Content of Human Milk." *Clinical Pediatrics* 17 (April 1978).

Pimentel, D., and Levitan, L. "Pesticides: Amounts Applied and Amounts Reaching Pests." *BioScience* 36 (February 1986): 86–91.

Potter, S., et al. "Does Infant Feeding Method Influence Maternal Postpartum Weight Loss?" *Journal of the American Dietetic Association* 91 (1991): 441–446.

Reeve, L.O., et al. "Vitamin D in Human Milk: Identification of Biologically Active Forms." *American Journal of Clinical Nutrition* 36, (July 1982).

Reeves, C.J.D. "Iron Supplementation in Infancy." *Pediatrics in Review* 8 (December 1986): 177–184.

Roberts, S.B., et al. "Energy Expenditure and Intake in Infants Born to Lean and Overweight Mothers." *The New England Journal of Medicine* 318 (February 1988): 461–466.

Rowe, J.C., et al. "Nutritional Hypophosphatenic Rickets in Premature Infants Fed Breast Milk." *The New England Journal of Medicine* 200 (1979).

Ruth, A.L. *Breastfeeding. A Guide for the Medical Profession.* St. Louis: C.V. Mosby Company, 1989.

Ruth, A.L. "Breast-Feeding." *Pediatrics in Review* 11 (December 1989): 163–171.

Ryan, A.S., and Martinez, G.A. "Breast-Feeding and the Working Mother: A Profile." *Pediatrics* 83 (April 1989): 524–531.

Saarinen, U.M., et al. "Iron Absorption in Infants." *Journal of Pediatrics* 91 (1977): 36–39.

Sugiyana, H., et al. "Number of Clostridium Botulism Spores in Honey." *Journal of Food Protection* 41 (1978).

Taubman, B. "Parental Counseling Compared with Elimination of Cow's Milk or Soy Milk Protein for the Treatment of Infant Colic Syndrome: A Randomized Trial." *Pediatrics* 81 (June 1988): 756–761.

Taylor, J.A., and Bergman, B.B. "Iron-Fortified Formulas: Pediatricians' Prescribing Practices." *Clinical Pediatrics* 28 (February 1989): 73–75.

Toufexis, A. "Watch What You Eat, Kid." *Time* (April 1991): 46.

Tsang, R.C., and Nichols, B.L. *Nutrition During Infancy*. Philadelphia: Hanley & Belfus, Inc., 1988.

Unger, R., et al. "Childhood Obesity." *Clinical Pediatrics* 29 (July 1990): 368–373.

USDA. "Composition of Baby Foods: Raw, Processed, Prepared." *Agricultural Handbook No. 8* (December 1978).

Weaver, L.T.; Ewing, G.; and Taylor, L.C. "The Bowel Habits of Milk-Fed Infants." *Journal of Pediatric Gastroenterology and Nutrition* 7 (1988): 568–571.

Weaver, L.T. "Review. Bowel Habits from Birth to Old Age." *Journal of Pediatric Gastroenterology and Nutrition* 7 (1988): 637–640.

Whichelow, M.J. "Success and Failure in Breast-Feeding in Relation to Energy Intake." *Proc. Soc.* 38 (1976).

Woolridge, M.W., and Fisher, C. "Infant Feeding. Colic, 'Overfeeding,' and Symptoms of Lactose Malabsorption in the Breast-Fed Baby: A Possible Artifact of Feed Management?" *The Lancet* (August 1988): 382–384.

Workshop on Current Issues in Feeding the Normal Infant. "Summary. The Early Feeds: Human Milk Versus Formula and Bovine Milk." *Pediatrics* 75 (supplement, January 1985): 157–159.

Yamauchi, Y., and Yamanouchi, I. "Breast-Feeding Frequency During the First 24 Hours After Birth in Full-Term Neonates." *Pediatrics* 86 (August 1990): 171–175.

Zoppi, G., et al. "Potential Complications in the Use of Wheat Bran for Constipation in Infancy." *Journal of Pediatric Gastroenterology and Nutrition* 1 (1982): 91–95.

Recipe Index

General Index